THE PURPOSE OF THE JUNIOR LEAGUE OF CHICAGO IS EXCLUSIVELY EDUCATIONAL AND CHARITABLE AND IS COMMITTED TO PROMOTING VOLUNTEERISM AND TO IMPROVING THE COMMUNITY THROUGH THE EFFECTIVE ACTION AND LEADERSHIP OF TRAINED VOLUNTEERS.

THE PROFIT REALIZED BY THE JUNIOR LEAGUE OF CHICAGO, INC.; FROM SALES OF *ONE MAGNIFICENT COOKBOOK* WILL BE USED FOR PROJECTS THE ORGANIZATION SUPPORTS IN THE CHICAGO COMMUNITY.

The Junior League
of Chicago
Presents

One Magnificent Cookbook

CREDITS

Additional copies of *One Magnificent
Cookbook* may be obtained by writing:
    One Magnificent Cookbook
    The Junior League of Chicago, Inc.
    1447 N. Astor Street
    Chicago, Illinois 60610

The Junior League of Chicago wishes to specially thank the following groups and individ-
uals involved in *One Magnificent Cookbook:*

Designer
KAREN R. GAFRICK
*Mobium Corporation for Design
and Communication
Chicago and New York*

Photographer
MEL WINER
Harling-Winer Graphics

Food Stylist
CARROLL BRENTON MICHALEK

Illustrator
STEVE MAYSE
Cindy Moran/Bill Rabin & Assoc.

Calligrapher
DICK JOYCE
Eaton & Iwen, Inc.

Printer
HART GRAPHICS
Austin, Texas

Composition
DESIGN TYPOGRAPHERS, INC.
Chicago, Illinois

Editorial Assistance
MOBIUM CORPORATION

SPONSORS

Tiffany & Co. *Chicago's 150th Birthday
    Party Brunch, page 24-25*
Marshall Field & Co. *Architectural
    Walking Tour Luncheon, page 28-29*
Saks Fifth Avenue *Day at Express-Way's
    Party, page 34-35*
Liberty of London *Magnificent Mile
    Shopping Spree Tea, page 40-41*
The Crate and Barrel *Air and Water
    Show Party on the Terrace, page 44-45*
Lord & Taylor *Art Institute Exhibit
    Opening Cocktail Party, page 52-53*
Bloomingdale's *Goodman Theatre
    Opening Night Dinner Party,
    page 56-57*
Waterford Wedgwood U.S.A. *River North
    Gallery Opening Late-Nite Supper,
    page 62-63*

THIS BOOK IS DEDICATED TO
MEMBERS OF THE JUNIOR LEAGUE
OF CHICAGO WHO DONATED THEIR
TIME AND TALENTS TO PRODUCE THIS
CULINARY SALUTE TO CHICAGO.

WE WOULD LIKE TO SPECIALLY
THANK AMANDA DEYOUNG, KAREN
"ZIG" SMITH, SUZANNE STEVENS,
CARROLL MICHALEK, MIMI BURKE,
NANCY LARUE, MARY KAY MCMAHON,
CONNIE TESKA, KAREN TAYLOR AND
HOPE POOR FOR THEIR EFFORTS
ON *ONE MAGNIFICIENT COOKBOOK.*

MARY ANN LILLIE and
LYNNE CLARK NORDHOFF
Co-Chairpersons

TABLE OF CONTENTS

Magnificent Recipes

One Magnificent Cookbook

INTRODUCTION

Chicago stands tall in many ways: skyscrapers by Mies Van Der Rohe, the legacy of Louis Sullivan, the Adler Planetarium, a fountain named Buckingham. World-class in every way, Chicago is its architecture, art galleries and museums, the Chicago Symphony Orchestra, the Magnificent Mile and its boutiques. All of which implies: Chicago is its people.

Like the city's cultural diversity, the tastes of Chicago are rich and varied. Here, deep-dish pizza made its American debut, and a Belgian invented shrimp de Jonghe. With Octoberfest observed each autumn, a downtown street is blocked off for the selling of bratwursts and beer. And everyday on State Street, curbside vendors delight the taste buds of workers and shoppers. Wherever the feast and whatever the fare, there is no dispute that Chicago cuisine is a distinct and delectable experience.

While some regard food as mere sustenance and eat to live, *One Magnificent Cookbook* is dedicated to those of us who live to eat. In addition to a collection of outstanding recipes, this book offers a medley of innovative ideas for successful entertaining. The pages that follow are filled with glorious excuses to throw a party and dishes certain to please. Collected here are the prized recipes of some of this city's most adept hostesses, members of the Junior League of Chicago. What these ladies know—and are known for—is graciousness in the grand Chicago tradition.

ENTERTAINING WITH CHICAGO FLAIR

The skyline's the limit for concocting your own fun in and around the Windy City, and this idea book from the Junior League of Chicago can help your imagination soar. Entertaining is a wonderful way to showcase your individual tastes and talents. As the host/hostess, you determine precisely what the tone of your party will be.

When deciding on the setting, keep in mind those things that make you most comfortable. You may not wish to have the party in your own home. Or, if you anticipate a need for assistance, you may want to hire a bartender or caterer.

Invitations should be mailed at least three to four weeks in advance, earlier for more formal affairs. The sooner you know how many people will attend, the better you'll be able to plan. If your get-together is casual, invite your friends over the telephone.

Check your linens and tableware well beforehand to make sure they are spotless and ready to go. Make arrangements for hired help early enough so you can go over critical details. Will the bartender provide the barware or use yours? Special drinks should reflect the ambience as well as the time of day and the season of the year. Choose music and flower arrangements that will enhance the mood you want to establish.

When your guests arrive, personally welcome them at the door with a smile and greeting, then make all necessary introductions. If you have a co-host, have him or her greet the guests with you and take their wraps. Your co-host can also supervise the bar and help serve the food later. If all this sounds complex and demanding, remember not to panic. Your company will be perfectly understanding of any last-minute food preparations. When you are able to break away from the kitchen, be a social butterfly and mingle as much as you can.

If you are well prepared, the logistics of your gala will be smooth, and you'll relax and enjoy yourself with the rest of the party-goers. Although you're giving the party and have many responsibilities, you should still have a good time! Entertaining can be a marvelously rewarding experience. The secret is readiness. Stay calm. After all, there's nothing to worry about—everything's under control!

One Magnificent Cookbook helps make your job easier by suggesting menus and themes. But only your personal flair and creativity can make these ideas work successfully.

MAGNIFICENT BRUNCHES

Whether casual or formal, brunches should progress at a leisurely pace. Sunday is the usual day for them, but why limit yourself to one day of the week? A brunch can follow a morning tennis match or precede an afternoon bridge game. Bring together as many friends as the sum of your rooms can comfortably accommodate.

Obviously the hour you choose will guide you in your food selection. An early brunch demands more breakfast dishes; served closer to noon, brunch can become a feast in which morning foods are incidental.

Bloody Marys are *de rigueur,* but a special fruit punch provides variety. Champagne is always welcome; and the later a brunch is, the more appropriate serving wine becomes. Prepare plenty of tea and coffee. For a change of pace, brew one or two herbal teas or lace a pot or two of coffee with cinnamon or almond extract. Cold mornings will warm to steaming apple cider or hot chocolate.

So that you, too, can enjoy your gathering, prepare as many dishes as you can in advance. Stock your bar and arrange your table the night before. Decide whether you'll be serving sit-down or buffet style. Finalize your decorations, and be sure to store flowers overnight in the refrigerator. Cut the stems again before you place them on the table. Above all, avoid cooking rites at dawn or tethering yourself to the kitchen after your guests arrive. It's you they've come to visit–be free for them.

CHICAGO BEARS BRUNCH

CRABMEAT SCRAMBLE
WITH VERMOUTH

ANGEL HAIR PASTA IN
RICOTTA CUSTARD

BAKED CURRIED TOMATOES

SEASONAL FRUIT WITH FABULOUS
FRUIT SAUCE

MORNING GLORY MUFFINS

Gather your favorite diehard Chicago Bears fans together and host a pre-game brunch. A brunch is a great way to energize the fans to cheer the team on to victory. Decorate your brunch table in the Bears colors of blue and orange. Bears pennants, posters and miniature footballs can add to the mood of your party. Use Bears mugs to serve coffee, and don't forget to wear your Bears T-shirt, jersey or jacket. Your invitation can even be decorated in blue and orange and/or feature the Bears insignia. After the brunch get ready to cheer for the home team!

....

BROCCOLI BUTTERMILK SOUP
WITH DILL

BAKED HAM WITH SHERRIED
MUSTARD SAUCE

VEGETABLE FRITTATA

STRAWBERRY SPINACH SALAD

MINI-PEACH MUFFINS

PERSIMMON PUDDING AND SAUCE

....

Chicago is 150 years old. What better way to celebrate than to throw a birthday brunch for this grand old city? Serve the food buffet-style with an ice sculpture of the city's skyline or possibly the Water Tower. Windy City souvenir items can serve as take-home table mementos or favors for your guests. Miniature city of Chicago flags or even colorful balloons can adorn your home for the special event. If you have any Chicago memorabilia, bring it out for show. This is a birthday bash; so celebrate!

CHICAGO'S 150TH BIRTHDAY PARTY BRUNCH
COURTESY OF TIFFANY & CO.

MAGNIFICENT LUNCHEONS

A luncheon can be magnificent any day of the week. If you wish it to be leisurely, schedule yours for a holiday or weekend. While a sit-down luncheon can last as long as a formal dinner, don't let that discourage you. If you know guests have business or other obligations, a buffet may be the wiser choice.

Set your table as you would for dinner. Choose place mats of linen, needlework or lace. Make sure your linens and tableware match the theme you have chosen. It's not necessary to clutter your table with extravagant decorations; a single stem of flowers at each place will do. When you are conscientious about pleasing your guests, you can't help but win their praise.

FORMAL LUNCHEON   PICTURED ON COVER
....

ICED STRAWBERRY SOUP

HALIBUT EN PAPILLOTE

HOT ASPARAGUS MOUSSE WITH
ORANGE SAUCE

RICE AND PINE NUTS

RIESLING ICE

....

A formal luncheon is an elegant way to visit with busy friends. Absorbed in numerous evening commitments, they will be grateful for a less-hectic interval in the afternoon. You'll want your luncheon to be sophisticated, so decorate with roses and light colors and bring out your best china, crystal and silver. Your goal should be to prepare a light but magnificent meal that will be the focal point of a special day.

ARCHITECTURAL WALKING TOUR LUNCHEON

GRUYÈRE PARMESAN PUFFS

CREAMY GINGER SHRIMP WITH
SPINACH PASTA

STEAMED PEA PODS AND
CARROT MATCHSTICKS*

ALMOND CRUMB BREAD

Early-morning architectural adventures in Chicago are ambitious endeavors that can give trekkers sore feet and hollow stomachs. After touring the works of Frank Lloyd Wright in west-suburban Oak Park or enjoying the myriad of works by eminent architects represented downtown, your guests will require respite and refueling.

Wouldn't it be pleasant if they could anticipate a refreshing luncheon at your place? You could decorate with posters and replicas of some the city's most famous architectural sights. And remember that colorful postcards can be transformed into clever place cards.

*Recipe not included in book.

ARCHITECTURAL WALKING TOUR LUNCHEON
COURTESY OF MARSHALL FIELD & CO.

BOTANIC GARDENS SPRING LUNCHEON

SPRING MINT, PEA AND
AVOCADO SOUP

GARDEN TOMATO PIE

STEAK SALAD WITH
MUSTARD VINAIGRETTE

THREE CHEESE BREAD

PERSIAN SLICES

With winter finally over, the promise of spring abounds! Everyone is eager to spend time outdoors after being cooped up indoors for so long. Where better to observe Mother Nature at her nurtured best than at the Chicago Botanic Gardens in Glencoe on the North Shore?

After touring the gardens all morning, your fellow plant lovers will look forward to lunchtime. You might plan a luncheon around one of the special events featured by the Gardens, such as the orchid or azalea show. You'll want to have an abundance of beautiful springtime flowers to keep that fresh smell of spring in the air. And decorating with bright, cheery colors will help you keep the mood carefree.

BASIL TOMATO SALAD WITH
SMOKED MOZZARELLA

HAZELNUT PESTO TURKEY BREAST

GENOA POLENTA WITH
WILD MUSHROOMS

GRILLED PEPPERS AND EGGPLANT

MACERATED ORANGES AND DATES
WITH PINE NUTS

In October, celebrate Columbus Day in style: Host a luncheon and parade-watching party honoring the New World's founder. Decorate with ribbons and balloons in red, white and green, and assemble a table centerpiece using festive fall flowers and miniature Italian flags. Try to recall an old history lesson and use it imaginatively.

MAGNIFICENT CHILDREN'S PARTIES

Teach children early, and hosting parties will never be the ordeal for them that it is for some. A party with their friends is an opportunity to practice the manners they've been taught and to have fun, too.

Having a theme is essential. Though children are easily pleased, they'll feel more comfortable if the surroundings are enjoyable. Make sure decorations are eye-catching and colorful. Plan activities that are age-appropriate—and plan plenty of them. For your own sake, limit the party to two to two-and-a-half hours and request that parents attend if children are under two years old.

Take care that no child appears left out of the festivities, and send each home with a party favor. Coloring books and small toys can be awarded to game winners. Since feelings are often tender, try to provide consolation prizes for those who do not win, or plan noncompetitive games or craft activities. Older children especially enjoy magicians, clowns, jugglers and mimes. If you can manage it, hire one for an hour. Whatever your child's age, be sure to include him or her in every facet of the party, from drafting the guest list to writing thank-you notes later.

CHECKERBOARD SANDWICHES

PEANUT BUTTER STICKS

MINI FRUIT KABOBS*

THE BEST CHOCOLATE CHUNK
MONSTER COOKIES...EVER

Express-Ways is a children's museum in Lincoln Park that offers kids (and adults) hands-on experience away from school. Here they can learn about everything from reading to art! Challenging mental and motor activity can develop big appetites in little kids, and you can reenergize them, prolonging their educational enthusiasm, by treating them to a special party afterwards. The children's museum creations would make terrific table decorations. And it would be a fun idea to carry over Express-Way's "five senses" theme into the party festivities—music can be *heard,* game objects can be *felt* and food can be *seen* as well as *smelled* and *tasted.*

Checkerboard sandwiches are fun to make. Two servings require two slices each of square-shaped white and wheat bread. You'll need to make one white and one wheat sandwich; so put your desired filling between the slices of bread. After removing the crusts, cut the sandwiches in quarters and arrange the light and dark squares on the tray to form a checkerboard pattern.

*Recipe not included in book.

DAY AT EXPRESS-WAYS PARTY
COURTESY OF SAKS FIFTH AVENUE

AFTER THE HOCKEY GAME PARTY

CHEESY VEGETABLE CHOWDER

HOCKEY STICK BREAD

BACON AND TOMATO
SALAD SANDWICHES

CHICAGO PEANUT BUTTER PIE

You can create edible miniature hockey sticks for your son and his teammates by twisting a simple yeast-dough recipe into bread sticks with angled ends. They're perfect for stirring into a mug of warm, cheesy vegetable chowder after your little guy's hockey practice or game on the hard, cold ice. Be sure to decorate with his team colors, and use hockey paraphernalia for table decorations and place cards. Keep the meal casual and the mood relaxed. Serve crumbled bacon, fresh spinach and tomato chunks tossed with bacon dressing on whole-wheat buns for tasty, nutritious sandwiches.

LITTLE GIRL'S "DRESS UP" PARTY

....

CHEDDAR CHEESE BOWS

PETIT CHICKEN SALAD SANDWICHES*

FRESH BERRIES WITH WHIPPED
ZABAGLIONE SAUCE

....

Little girls love to dress up in mom's clothes and play make-believe.
Why not let your daughter carry her fantasy one step closer to reality
by imitating a formal luncheon that you might have? Live entertain-
ment, such as the Madhatters acting troupe, is a possibility, but must
be kept prim and proper because the young ladies will be on their
best behavior in their finest apparel. In addition to decorating with
flowers, you may wish to pin pretty corsages on your mini-hostess
and her youthful guests. Old-fashioned macaroni and cheese takes
on a new, feminine flair when bow-shaped pasta is used.

*Recipe not included in book.

MAGNIFICENT AFTERNOON TEA

For most Americans, afternoon tea is a familiar ritual from British murder mysteries. While a homegrown sleuth like Sam Spade would sooner die of heartbreak than nibble scones and take milk with tea, American attitudes have changed. Today more than one generation embraces this simplest—and most civilized—excuse to socialize.

Like dinner parties, afternoon tea can range from informal get-togethers to extremely formal events. Have the neighbors over and, unless you're new in the neighborhood, you need not make a fuss nor send out invitations; the phone will do. If you're honoring a special person, send formal notes to your guests.

Reserve your daintiest linens for serving tea, and do remember that tea itself refers not only to the drink but to the delicacies that accompany it. Arrange your refreshments—for that is what the English consider tea to be—on a buffet table, a sideboard or, if you're truly committed, on a special tea table.

Include a few exotic teas along with traditional flavors. Since many Americans have not yet warmed to the idea of milk in tea, be sure to provide lemon slices along with sugar lumps and honey. Coffee, hot chocolate, hot cider or mulled wine may also be served. Traditional tea favorites include scones, fruit tartlets, finger sandwiches, cakes, breads, fresh fruit and spreads made from meat, fish or cheese.

The beauty of giving a tea is that once your table is set, your work is largely over. You can greet guests, make appropriate introductions, pour their beverages and enjoy the company.

ENGLISH TEA SANDWICHES

STRAWBERRY BREAD

LEMON TEA BREAD

BLUEBERRY SCONES WITH
CLOTTED CREAM

ASSORTED FANCY COOKIES*

FRESH STRAWBERRIES*

North Michigan Avenue's "Magnificent Mile" is home to some of the finest retail shops in the world. Finding even the most obscure and elegant item is usually a matter of simply looking in the right place. And there are oh so many places to browse—department stores, jewelers, fur salons, boutiques.

Wind down an exhausting day of shopping downtown with a relaxing late-afternoon tea for your friends. Be sure to bring out your fancy linens, brew a variety of teas and serve an assortment of savories and sweets.

*Recipe not included in book.

MAGNIFICENT MILE SHOPPING SPREE TEA
COURTESY OF LIBERTY OF LONDON

MAGNIFICENT OUTDOOR PARTIES

Chicago on a balmy day is the perfect setting for an outdoor gathering. Whether you choose your patio, a park, the lakefront or your sailboat, make sure you've an alternate plan in the event the weather doesn't cooperate. Prearrange a rain date and make it known beforehand, or plan to move your guests indoors. A tent is also a good choice for outdoor entertaining.

Several hours before the guests arrive, spray the party area with insect repellent or fasten citronella candles just outside the perimeter of it. Because pests are inevitable, monitor the table once the food is in place. Serving trays with covers are often useful outdoors.

Decorating for an outdoor event is unnecessary if you are careful in selecting your setting – nature does the work. If not lakeside, perhaps you could arrange a garden or woodsy view. If you must decorate, decide on a theme and choose colorful table settings to convey it. Plan any sports or games to coincide with the theme you choose – but don't let activities interfere with your meal. For formal events like graduations and christenings, an unusual centerpiece can be the focal point of your table.

Depending on how formal your party is, seating can range from a patchwork of blankets to lawn chairs and tiny tables. Make certain that ample seating is available for all your guests – placed so they are free to mix and mingle.

Let your imagination run wild. The location you choose and the food you serve will guarantee the pleasures of a summer party.

CROUTONS WITH THREE CHEESES
AND SUN-DRIED TOMATOES

GRILLED PORK CHOPS WITH
ARUGULA BUTTER

FRESH CORN ON THE GRILL*

MARINATED VEGETABLE SALAD WITH
DIJON DRESSING

FRESH APPLE CAKE WITH
PENUCHE FROSTING

The incredible Air and Water Show attracts millions of spectators to Chicago's lakefront every summer. You can throw a fabulous pre- or post-show party on your terrace, or, if your terrace offers an exquisite view of the remarkable stunts, hold your party during the show. You'll probably want to decorate with an aviation/naval theme in blue and white. Because you'll be outside, keep the tableware and linens casual, or consider serving the food indoors while reserving your terrace for eating and admiring the view.

*Recipe not included in book.

AIR AND WATER SHOW PARTY ON THE TERRACE
COURTESY OF THE CRATE AND BARREL

EARLY DINNER BEFORE JAZZ FEST
IN GRANT PARK

....

CUCUMBER TOMATO SOUP

GRILLED SOFT-SHELL CRAB IN
BASIL MARINADE

FRESH TRI-COLOR PASTA
AND PARMESAN*

THREE PEA MÉLANGE

ICE CREAM IN TULIP COOKIES TOPPED
WITH MISSISSIPPI MUD SAUCE

....

An early dinner is a fine prélude to Chicago's annual Jazz Fest. The setting could be your backyard or terrace, or, if your menu is simpler, the north end of Grant Park itself. Just pack a picnic basket, toss a blanket over your shoulder and meet some friends in front of the Petrillo Band Shell near Monroe Street and Columbus Drive. Bring along nonperishable food that's ready to eat when you arrive. Wherever you decide to serve your delicious meal, you and your guests will be ready to sit back, relax and listen to the swingin' sounds of some of the world's best jazz artists.

*Recipe not included in book.

CHICAGO'S MARATHON SALAD BUFFET

BEEF, PEPPER AND AVOCADO SALAD

ORIENTAL CHICKEN SALAD

SHRIMP AND VEGETABLE SALAD

POTATO SALAD WITH
SMOKED SALMON

BULGUR AND KASHA SALAD

FRECKLED PEPPER CHEESE BREAD

WALNUT WHEAT BREAD

BLACKBERRY PLUM PIE

CHOCOLATE CHIP WALNUT PIE

FRESH MELON WEDGES*

Preparing a crisp salad buffet is a healthy way to inspire the marathoner in your life. And even if you don't personally know anyone going the distance, a marathon is cause to celebrate human endurance. While Chicago's Marathon participants are running through the city's ethnic neighborhoods, you can escort your guests on a culinary tour featuring salads of diverse origins. Nutrition is the key here, so be sure to have plenty of fruit juices, water and other beverages on hand.

*Recipe not included in book.

FOURTH OF JULY SAILING PARTY

··

COLD PORK PITA POCKETS WITH
BEAN SPROUTS

FRENCH POTATO SALAD

ASPARAGUS WITH
CHINESE VINAIGRETTE

RASPBERRY WALNUT SNOW BARS

··

The opportunity to watch Chicago's breathtaking Fourth of July fireworks from a sailboat on Lake Michigan should not be taken for granted. Not only will you have the best vantage point in the city, but you won't have to wrestle with the crowds. Be sure to bring a wide range of beverages; it's likely to be hot and humid until the pleasant lake breezes cool things off at sunset. The fare should include a variety of finger foods suitable for munching all day long. Serve supper before the show booms to life so your friends can "ooh" and "aah" as the skyline explodes with brilliant color.

MAGNIFICENT COCKTAIL PARTIES

Consider a cocktail party for the opportunity it represents: the chance to entertain far more guests than you could ever seat for dinner. While dinner conversation is liveliest when interests are compatible, the reverse is true of the cocktail party. Bring people of various pursuits together, and a successful evening is nearly assured.

Ready an equal balance of hot and cold foods. Be creative but serve your selections in bite-size portions since guests must manage both food and drink while standing.

Hire servers if you'd like, or prepare a buffet table and invite people to serve themselves. Choose whichever method makes the most sense based on the size of your party and the variety of food you wish to serve.

Securing a bartender is a worthy idea and frees you and your guests from mixing the drinks. Make sure you have the appropriate barware, along with a generous supply of ice, soft drinks, juices, liquor, wine, champagne and beer. Provide plenty of nonalcoholic beverages for those who prefer not to imbibe.

A cocktail party can be thrown without reason, but if you'd prefer one, plan it before a gala or the opening of a new exhibit. In any event, it need not be longer than two or three hours. Fresh flowers are always appropriate. Candles, silver and linens will formalize the affair. By bringing many people together, your party will inevitably be the start of some new friendships; this in itself is reason to celebrate!

ART INSTITUTE EXHIBIT OPENING
COCKTAIL PARTY

PICTURED

PÂTÉ WITH GOAT CHEESE

SALMON DILL
CUCUMBER SANDWICHES

EGGPLANT SANDWICHES

FIESTA CHICKEN WITH YOGURT AND
CUCUMBER DIP

SHRIMP AND TORTELLINI SALAD
WITH BASIL

SHORE SCALLOPS WITH
AVOCADO BUTTER

SHAVED TURKEY AND HAM WITH
ASSORTED MAYONNAISES
AND MUSTARDS*

PECAN CHOCOLATE
BUTTERSCOTCH BARS

LEMON COCONUTTY SQUARES

The Art Institute of Chicago is home to the work of some of the
world's finest artists, and its special exhibits are musts for art
aficionados. Invite your friends to play art critic at a pre-exhibit

cocktail party. For decorations, the museum store may sell replicas of the exhibit pieces you expect to see later that evening. You might also be able to find napkins and linens in an artwork design. You can add a touch of elegance to your special gathering with fresh flowers and candles—the anticipation of the opening will provide the excitement.

*Recipe not included in book.

BLACK TIE PRE-GALA COCKTAIL PARTY

ARTICHOKE AND SHRIMP APPETIZER

SUGAR AND NUT GLAZED BRIE

QUESADILLAS WITH MORELS

CRAB AVOCADO CANAPÉS

A black-tie gala represents city living at its finest. Begin the magnificent evening with a cocktail party in your home. Set out your finest china, crystal and silver, as well as flowers and candles, to make a spectacular, formal setting for your food. Everyone will leave in a lively mood, and the festivities will continue at the main event.

ART INSTITUTE EXHIBIT OPENING COCKTAIL PARTY
COURTESY OF LORD & TAYLOR

MAGNIFICENT DINNER PARTIES

If three is company and two none, as Oscar Wilde presumed the state of marriage to be, then what of the dinner party? How many is adequate company? And should you really insist on pairing your guests? While a dinner party is the most common form of entertaining, it can still prove baffling.

As relaxed as proprieties have become, the dinner party remains an elegant affair, and there are many who relish its formality. How many guests you seat depends on how many you can comfortably accommodate. Having an even number of guests makes it convenient at the table. Place cards will guide your guests to their seats.

And what of the fare? Plan a meal balanced in color and texture. If you serve hors d'oeuvres with cocktails, be sure they are not too filling. If your guests don't know one another, a cocktail hour is a good way to encourage them to get acquainted before moving in to dinner.

Think you need extra help? Hire servers. Insist that plates be served to your guests from the left and removed from the right. After the main course, the table should be cleared of dinner, salad and butter plates, condiment dishes and salt and pepper shakers.

Coffee and dessert may be served at the table or removed to the terrace or the living room. Do offer your guests after-dinner liqueurs and nonalcoholic beverages. To encourage conversation, don't allow the music to be louder than a murmur. Remember, the success of your party depends on how sensitive you are to the details of the setting as well as to your guests.

GOODMAN THEATRE OPENING NIGHT DINNER PARTY

PICTURED

....

SOUP VERTE

VEAL ROLL WITH APRICOTS
IN CALVADOS

WILD RICE WITH ALMONDS
AND MUSHROOMS

HERBED GREEN BEANS*

GINGER SOUFFLÉ WITH
CHOCOLATE SAUCE

....

Before driving to the Goodman for the opening night of its latest play, host an elegant dinner celebration for your fellow theatre-goers. As a formal affair, your décor should be simple. For a creative accent, print your menu in the style of a playbill. The food is the star of this production, and you'll want to make sure it receives rave reviews. Break a leg!

*Recipe not included in book.

GOODMAN THEATRE OPENING NIGHT DINNER PARTY
COURTESY OF BLOOMINGDALE'S

"I LOVE CHICAGO" DINNER PARTY

··

ARUGULA AND PINE NUT SALAD WITH
CONFETTI DRESSING

POACHED SALMON GOOD WITH
CAPER SAUCE

STEAMED BABY ARTICHOKES AND
RED POTATOES

CHAMPAGNE POACHED PEARS

··

Whether your guests are native Chicagoans or out-of-towners, you can declare your love for what poet Carl Sandburg called the "City of Big Shoulders" with a dinner party. Which of Chicago's sights and attractions do you like best? This question can be the catalyst for lively dinner discussion. Purchase Windy City memorabilia for decorations, and play appropriate music about the city ("My kind of town…," "Chicago, Chicago…") and from the city (blues).

NEW YEAR'S EVE BLACK TIE DINNER PARTY

MARINATED SALMON WITH
CAVIAR DRESSING

CHAMPAGNE ROASTED
CORNISH HENS

ORZO PASTA WITH WATERCRESS*

ASPARAGUS WITH RED
PEPPER HOLLANDAISE

BLACKBERRY ICE

Celebrate the new year's arrival in style with a refined and sophisticated black-tie dinner party. Set your table with splendid crystal and
silverware, then reminisce about unkept resolutions over sumptu-
ous provisions. Have plenty of champagne on ice for the traditional
midnight toast. You'll want to make your feast so distinctive that one
of your friends' resolutions will be to attend an equally special
event next December 31st.

*Recipe not included in book.

MAGNIFICENT LATE-NIGHT SUPPERS

Late suppers have long been the hallmark of privilege. Jay Gatsby gave them, John Held drew them and Frank Capra filmed them. Since the Jazz Age, writers, artists and Hollywood directors have romanticized one invitation above others–dinner after ten.

Following Lyric Opera, the Chicago Ballet or a gallery opening in River North, a late supper is a fitting way to continue the evening. Conversation can focus on the evening and upcoming events. A late supper is a means of bringing together those who meet all too infrequently. And it is always elegant.

A late-night supper is entertaining with the utmost confidence. An extension of your evening, it means planning every detail hours before you return with your guests. Because of its lateness, the meal should be light. You decide whether hors d'oeuvres are necessary based on the time you need to finalize dinner. Invite guests to fix their own drinks from a well-stocked bar (which should include nonalcoholic beverages, such as soft drinks and sparkling water), and play appropriate music to help them unwind.

More than a gracious end to an evening, hosting a late-night supper is the ultimate gesture of hospitality. It takes some thought and careful planning, but is a splendid way to end an evening on a high note.

CHICAGO FISH CHOWDER

CAMEMBERT FRENCH BREAD

ARUGULA RADICCHIO AND MUSTARD
SPROUT SALAD

CHOCOLATE PRALINE PUMPKIN PIE

Red-brick loft buildings with hardwood floors and exposed wooden beams give the illusion that time has stood still in the area a mile west of Lake Michigan's shoreline. Shiny skyscrapers rise across the Chicago River, but this neighborhood ignores their intimidating presence, maintaining a nostalgia all its own. River North's renovated warehouses, the one-time backbone of Chicago's great manufacturing monopoly, are the vibrant new homes of businesses, fine restaurants and art galleries.

Gallery exhibit openings occur frequently and offer the opportunity for an urbane soirée. After viewing the work of a prominent or emerging artist, have your "critics" over for drinks and a wonderful late-night supper.

RIVER NORTH GALLERY OPENING LATE-NIGHT SUPPER
COURTESY OF WATERFORD WEDGWOOD U.S.A.

LYRIC OPERA OPENING LATE-NIGHT SUPPER

WATERCRESS AND WATER
CHESTNUT SALAD

HAZELNUT PORK CUTLETS WITH PORT
WINE SAUCE

BUTTERED SPAETZLE*

TRI-COLOR VEGETABLES

WINTER CARNIVAL FRUIT COMPOTE

After an enchanting black-tie opening at Chicago's Lyric Opera, host
an equally formal late-night supper. Prepare in advance special
entrées that will excite your guests' taste buds in the same way that
the music delighted their ears! Keep the table setting formal, and
cleverly design your invitation in the form of an operatic libretto.
*Recipe not included in book.

SECOND CITY "AFTER THE REVIEW" LATE-NIGHT SUPPER

....

POTTED HERB CHEESE

CHICKEN WITH LIME BUTTER SAUCE

PARSLIED RICE*

SPICY BROCCOLI WITH TOMATOES

FRESH STUFFED PEACHES

....

Second City historically spotlights the funniest up-and-coming comedians in the country. Any of the hilarious revues could be the unveiling of the next comedic star. After an uproarious evening filled with inventive live comedy and improvisation, retreat to your house for a late-night supper. Set the stage by using souvenirs from Second City as props, and lead your guests into the first skit with drinks and appetizers. Then, put the finishing touches on your repast (remember, this is the real thing, not a dress rehearsal), and enjoy the night's grand finale.

*Recipe not included in book.

Magnificent Recipes

THE ADLER PLANETARIUM is named for its donor, Max Adler, a former vice president of Sears Roebuck & Co. Built in 1931 on the shores of Lake Michigan, this granite-domed structure is highlighted by a series of reflecting pools leading to its entrance. An underground wing was added in 1975 to house exhibits on space exploration. The museum contains one of the world's finest collections of antique astronomical and mathematical instruments.

2	FRESH ARTICHOKES
	VEGETABLE OIL
4	OUNCES SOUR CREAM
1	TEASPOON WORCHESTERSHIRE
	SAUCE
1	DROP HOT RED PEPPER SAUCE
½	TEASPOON CELERY SALT
½	TEASPOON GARLIC SALT
½	POUND FRESH BAY SHRIMP,
	COOKED, SHELLS REMOVED
	PAPRIKA

ARTICHOKE AND SHRIMP APPETIZER

Cut off artichoke tops and sharp leaf tips with scissors. Stand artichokes in several inches of water to which a little vegetable oil has been added. Steam until tender, about 25-30 minutes. Cool. Separate leaves.

Mix sour cream with Worcestershire sauce, red pepper sauce, celery salt and garlic salt.

Put a dab of mixture on meaty end of each artichoke leaf and place a shrimp on top.

Sprinkle with paprika to taste. Serve at room temperature. *Yield: 6 to 8 servings.*

10	CUPS CHICKEN BROTH
2	WHOLE CHICKEN BREASTS,
	BONED AND SKINNED
2	SCALLIONS
1	EGG
¼	CUP FRESHLY GRATED
	PARMESAN CHEESE
6	SPRIGS ITALIAN PARSLEY
2	CARROTS, JULIENNED
1	ZUCCHINI, JULIENNED
½	CUP CELERY ROOT, JULIENNED

CHICKEN CUSTARD WITH JULIENNED VEGETABLES

Preheat oven to 350° F. In a saucepan bring chicken broth to simmer. Add breasts and poach 20 minutes or until juices run clear when pierced in the thickest part. Remove with slotted spoon and set aside, reserving broth.

In a food processor combine scallions, 1 whole chicken breast, ⅓ cup broth, egg, cheese and parsley. Process until smooth.

Scrape purée into 4 buttered 3″ x 2½″ timbale molds (or small soufflé dishes) and place in baking pan. Add enough warm water to pan to come halfway up sides of molds. Bake for 15 minutes or until knife tip inserted into center of molds comes out clean.

In a saucepan bring remaining broth to a simmer; add carrots, zucchini and celery root. Slice remaining breast into thin strips and add to broth. Simmer until vegetables are crisp-tender and chicken is heated through.

To serve, unmold cooked custard into soup bowls and ladle broth, vegetables and sliced chicken over custard. *Yield: 4 servings.*

18	LARGE FRESH ASPARAGUS SPEARS, PEELED
3	EGGS
2⅓	CUPS CRÈME FRAÎCHE
	SALT AND FRESHLY GROUND PEPPER
¾	CUP FRESH, SHELLED BABY PEAS
2	TABLESPOONS CHOPPED ONION
4	TABLESPOONS UNSALTED BUTTER
	PINCH CURRY POWDER
3	SLICES BREAD, TOASTED, HALVED AND CRUSTS REMOVED

ASPARAGUS FLANS

Preheat oven to 325° F. Trim asparagus spears to equal lengths. Tie in a bunch with a string. In a saucepan bring 2 quarts unsalted water to a boil. Stand spears in water with tips extending just above water line. Simmer until tender. Refresh, drain well. Trim off tips and set aside.

In a food processor combine asparagus stems, eggs and 1 cup of the crème fraîche. Process until smooth. Strain and season with salt and pepper to taste. Turn into 6 buttered dariole molds or 4-ounce ramekins.

Place molds in a roasting pan and fill pan with enough water to come halfway up sides of molds. Bake for 30 minutes or until knife tip inserted into center of molds comes out clean.

For sauce, in a small saucepan bring salted water to a boil. Add peas and boil 3 minutes. Refresh; drain well.

In a skillet, sauté onion in 2 tablespoons of the butter until softened. Add curry powder and remaining crème fraîche. Season with salt and pepper; simmer 3 minutes.

Process cream mixture, peas and remaining butter in food processor until smooth.

Divide sauce among six plates. Unmold flans and place in center of each plate. Garnish each with 3 asparagus tips (reheated if desired) and a toast triangle. *Yield: 6 servings.*

¼ CUP FIRMLY PACKED
  BROWN SUGAR
¼ CUP BROKEN WALNUTS, PECANS,
  MACADAMIA NUTS, ALMONDS
  OR HAZELNUTS
1 TABLESPOON BRANDY
1 14-OUNCE ROUND BRIE CHEESE
  FRESHLY SQUEEZED
  LEMON JUICE
  APPLE WEDGES, SEEDLESS
  GRAPES AND CRACKERS

SUGAR AND NUT GLAZED BRIE

In a small mixing bowl stir together sugar, nuts and brandy. Cover and chill thoroughly. *Preheat oven to 500° F.*

Place Brie on oven-proof serving platter. Bake for 4-5 minutes or until cheese is slightly softened. Sprinkle sugar-nut mixture over top; bake 2-3 minutes longer until sugar is melted and cheese is heated through but not melted.

Brush apple wedges with lemon juice to avoid discoloration. Arrange fruit and crackers around cheese. Serve immediately. *Yield: 16 to 20 servings.*

2 TABLESPOONS UNFLAVORED
  GELATIN
2 TABLESPOONS WATER
2 TABLESPOONS FRESHLY
  SQUEEZED LEMON JUICE
1¾ CUPS WHIPPING
  CREAM, CHILLED
2 LARGE RIPE AVOCADOS, PEELED,
  PITTED, COARSELY CHOPPED
  PINCH OF SALT
  WHITE PEPPER TO TASTE
10 OUNCES SLICED SMOKED
  SALMON
1 EGG WHITE
  SPINACH DIJON MAYONNAISE
  (SEE RECIPE IN
  SAUCE SECTION)
  FRESH PARSLEY AS GARNISH

TERRINE OF AVOCADO WITH SMOKED SALMON

Line a 5-cup terrine with plastic wrap, leaving enough to cover the top.

In a small bowl sprinkle the gelatin over the water and lemon juice. When liquid is absorbed, dissolve gelatin by placing the dish in a pan of hot water. Cool slightly.

Whip 1¼ cups of the cream until it holds soft peaks. Set aside.

Combine avocados, dissolved gelatin, salt and pepper in a food processor and purée. Gently fold into whipping cream. Adjust seasonings to taste. Set aside.

In a food processor purée 7 ounces of the salmon, then slowly add egg white and remaining ½ cup cream. Mix until smooth.

In terrine, place ⅓ of the avocado mixture and then ½ of the salmon mixture. Spread the last 3 ounces of sliced salmon in a single layer on top of the salmon mousse. Continue layering with ⅓ of the avocado, ½ of the salmon mousse and ⅓ of the avocado. Thump terrine on counter edge to settle mixture. Cover tightly with oiled plastic wrap and chill approximately 6 hours.

To serve, remove mold by inverting onto a flat platter. Smooth the surface and garnish with Spinach Dijon mayonnaise and parsley or cut into slices and serve on separate plates with same garnish. *Yield: 8 servings.*

12	OUNCES CREAM CHEESE, SOFTENED
¼	CUP FRESHLY GRATED PARMESAN CHEESE
1	TABLESPOON MINCED GARLIC
3	TEASPOONS MINCED FRESH BASIL
½	TEASPOON SALT
¼	TEASPOON FRESHLY GROUND PEPPER
1	TEASPOON EXTRA VIRGIN OLIVE OIL
7	SLICES PROVOLONE, ⅛″ THICK
⅔	CUP PINE NUTS
12	OUNCES MOZZARELLA, SLICED ¼″ THICK
	ITALIAN PARSLEY AS GARNISH

BASIL AND PROVOLONE TORTA

In a bowl beat cream cheese until fluffy. Add Parmesan cheese, garlic, basil, salt and pepper. Blend well.

Brush a 3-cup loaf pan with ½ teaspoon of the olive oil. Line the pan with plastic wrap leaving a 1″ overlap and brush wrap with remaining oil.

Spread ¼ cup of cheese mixture in bottom of pan. Trim 2 slices of Provolone to fit pan in a single layer and place on top of cheese mixture. Spread Provolone with ¼ cup cheese mixture. Arrange ¼ cup pine nuts over cheese in even lengthwise rows. Spread 2 tablespoons cheese mixture over nuts to cover.

Trim half of the mozzarella slices to fit in a single layer and place on top of cheese mixture. Spread mozzarella slices with 2 table-spoons cheese mixture. Add remaining mozzarella trimmed to fit pan. Spread mozzarella with half remaining cheese mixture. Top with remaining 5 slices of Provolone, trimmed to fit pan.

Wrap and refrigerate remaining cheese mixture. Cover torta with plastic wrap. Refrigerate for 12 hours.

One hour before unmolding, bring remaining cheese mixture to room temperature.

To unmold loaf, invert pan and tap edges. If loaf does not unmold, gently pull ends of plastic. Remove plastic and spread remaining cheese mixture over sides of loaf. Serve chilled, garnished with Italian parsley. *Yield: 1 loaf.*

16	OUNCES CREAM CHEESE, SOFTENED
¼	CUP BUTTER, SOFTENED
1	TABLESPOON MILK
2	CLOVES GARLIC, MINCED
1	TEASPOON CARAWAY SEED
1	TEASPOON PAPRIKA
2	TEASPOONS DIJON MUSTARD
½	TEASPOON ANCHOVY PASTE
	BIBB LETTUCE CUPS
	SLICED RIPE OLIVES
	SLICED RED ONION
	CRISP BACON PIECES
	CAPERS
	SLICED DILL PICKLES
	COCKTAIL RYE OR PUMPERNICKEL BREAD

SPICED CHEESE SPREAD WITH CONDIMENTS

Beat together cream cheese, butter and milk until smooth. Stir in garlic, caraway seed, paprika, mustard and anchovy paste. Cover and chill at least 8 hours.

Mound cheese spread on large platter. Surround with small lettuce cups filled with olives, onion, bacon, capers and dill pickles. Serve with the bread. *Yield: 2½ cups.*

8	OUNCES BONELESS, SKINLESS CHICKEN BREAST
2	EGG WHITES
⅛	TEASPOON MACE
½	TEASPOON CAYENNE PEPPER
¼	TEASPOON SALT
½	TEASPOON FRESHLY GROUND PEPPER
½	CUP SOUR CREAM
½	CUP CHOPPED PARSLEY
4	TABLESPOONS CHOPPED CHIVES
1	TEASPOON CRUSHED TARRAGON
½	CUP WHIPPING CREAM, WHIPPED UNTIL SOFT PEAKS FORM
3-4	SLICES HAM, JULIENNED

HERBED CHICKEN TERRINE

Preheat oven to 350° F. Combine chicken, egg whites, mace, cayenne, salt and pepper in food processor. Purée until smooth. Add sour cream, parsley, chives and tarragon and process until smooth.

Transfer mixture to large bowl and fold in whipped cream. Put half of mixture in buttered terrine or small loaf pan. Cover with ham strips. Top with remaining half of mixture and pack firmly.

Cover terrine with foil. Place terrine in large roasting pan and fill pan with hot water halfway up sides of terrine. Bake for 1 hour.

Unmold, slice and serve hot with hollandaise sauce or chill and serve with mayonnaise. *Yield: 6 servings.*

½	CUP MINCED ONION
1	TABLESPOON EXTRA VIRGIN OLIVE OIL
6	OUNCES SORREL LEAVES, SLICED INTO FINE STRIPS
1	CUP SOUR CREAM
½	CUP PLAIN YOGURT
1	HARD-COOKED EGG, CHOPPED
2	POUNDS SHRIMP IN THE SHELL, COOKED AND COOLED

SHRIMP WITH SORREL SAUCE

In a skillet, cook onion in oil until soft. Add sorrel leaves and cook over low heat stirring occasionally, about 10 minutes or until sorrel is softened. Remove from heat.

Combine cooled sorrel with sour cream, yogurt and egg.

Serve chilled as a dip for shrimp. *Yield: 1¾ cups sauce.*

2	POUNDS, BONELESS, SKINLESS CHICKEN BREASTS CUT INTO 50 LARGE, BITE-SIZE PIECES
	MARINADE
2½	CUPS PLAIN YOGURT
¼	TEASPOON CHILI POWDER
¼	TEASPOON GROUND CUMIN
¼	TEASPOON GROUND CORIANDER
4	TEASPOONS CURRY POWDER
4	TEASPOONS TOMATO PASTE
	JUICE AND GRATED RIND OF 2 LEMONS
4	CLOVES GARLIC, FINELY CHOPPED
4	TEASPOONS FRESH GINGER ROOT, FINELY CHOPPED
	SALT AND FRESHLY GROUND PEPPER TO TASTE
	DIP
2	CUCUMBERS, FINELY CHOPPED, SQUEEZED AND PATTED LIGHTLY ON PAPER TOWELS TO EXTRACT MOISTURE
2½	CUPS PLAIN YOGURT
¼	CUP WHIPPING CREAM
¼	CUP FINELY CHOPPED FRESH MINT
	SALT AND FRESHLY GROUND PEPPER TO TASTE

FIESTA CHICKEN WITH CUCUMBER AND YOGURT DIP

In a food processor combine all marinade ingredients and process until smooth.

For the dip, combine all ingredients, cover and chill.

Place chicken into a large nonaluminum bowl and pour marinade over. Cover and chill 6 hours. *Preheat oven to 500° F.*

Remove chicken from marinade and arrange in a single layer in a large roasting pan.

Cook chicken about 10 minutes or until reddish brown and tender. Transfer it to a serving platter.

Serve chicken hot with bowl of dip and large cocktail picks.

Yield: approximately 25 appetizers

1   SHEET PUFF PASTRY, ABOUT
        8 OUNCES
1   EGG
1   TABLESPOON WATER
¼   CUP MAYONNAISE
1   TABLESPOON FRESHLY
        SQUEEZED LEMON JUICE
¼   TEASPOON GRATED LEMON PEEL
⅛   TEASPOON HOT RED
        PEPPER SAUCE
10 OUNCES CRABMEAT
        SALT AND FRESHLY
        GROUND PEPPER
2   AVOCADOS, PEELED, PITTED
        AND THINLY SLICED
        (24 SLICES)
8   CHERRY TOMATOES, SLICED
        INTO THIRDS

CRAB AVOCADO CANAPÉS

Preheat oven to 400° F. On floured surface roll out puff pastry to a 12″ square. Cut into four 3″ strips; place on a large ungreased baking sheet. Beat together egg and water; brush on pastry.

Prick pastry thoroughly with a fork. Bake 10-12 minutes or until puffed and lightly browned. Cool on wire rack.

In a medium bowl combine mayonnaise, lemon juice, lemon peel and hot red pepper sauce; stir in crabmeat. Season to taste with salt and pepper.

When pastry is cool, cut each strip into 6 pieces. Arrange avocado slice on pastry. Place tomato slice and crab mixture on top. Sprinkle each hors d'oeuvre with pepper and serve immediately. *Yield: 24 hors d'oeuvres.*

1   FRENCH BREAD BAGUETTE, CUT
        INTO ¼″ SLICES
        EXTRA VIRGIN OLIVE OIL
¼   POUND CALIFORNIA GOAT
        CHEESE WITH HERBS
¼   POUND RICOTTA CHEESE
¼   POUND MOZZARELLA
        CHEESE, SHREDDED
1   LARGE GARLIC CLOVE, MINCED
        WHITE PEPPER
18 SUN-DRIED TOMATOES,
        DRAINED AND HALVED

CROUTONS WITH THREE CHEESES AND SUN-DRIED TOMATOES

Preheat oven to 300° F. Arrange bread slices on baking sheet. Brush tops with olive oil. Bake until croutons are golden brown, about 2 minutes. Remove from oven and set aside. *Increase oven temperature to 350° F.*

Blend cheeses and garlic in a bowl. Season with pepper. Mound 1 teaspoon cheese mixture on each crouton. Top with sun-dried tomato half. Cover with an additional 1 teaspoon cheese mixture.

Bake until cheese begins to melt. Serve immediately. *Yield: 36 appetizers.*

16	LARGE ESCARGOTS
1	CUP COGNAC
1	SHEET PUFF PASTRY, ABOUT 12 OUNCES
2	OUNCES PÂTÉ DE FOIE GRAS, CUT INTO 4 THIN SLICES
2	EGG YOLKS, BEATEN

ESCARGOTS AND PÂTÉ IN PUFF PASTRY

Preheat oven to 400° F. Marinate escargots in cognac for 6-8 hours.

Roll out puff pastry to ⅛″ thickness. Cut into 4 rounds, each about 3½″ in diameter.

Place 4 escargots on half of each pastry round.

Arrange slices of pâté on top of escargots. Brush edges of pastry rounds with egg yolks. Fold each round in half, like a half moon. Press edges together to seal. Brush with egg yolks and bake 5-7 minutes or until golden brown. *Yield: 4 servings.*

1	CUP MILK
8	TABLESPOONS UNSALTED BUTTER
½	TEASPOON SALT
	PINCH OF WHITE PEPPER
1	CUP SIFTED FLOUR
5	EGGS
1¼	CUPS GRATED PARMESAN CHEESE
¾	CUP GRATED GRUYÈRE CHEESE

GRUYÈRE PARMESAN PUFFS

Preheat oven to 350° F. In a large saucepan combine milk, butter, salt and pepper and bring to a boil. Remove pan from heat, add flour and whisk vigorously. Return pan to heat and cook, stirring constantly, until batter has thickened and pulls away from sides of pan.

Remove pan from heat. Add 4 of the eggs, one at a time, thoroughly mixing batter before another egg is added. Stir in ¾ cup of the Parmesan and all of the Gruyère.

Drop the batter by tablespoons onto a buttered baking sheet, placing them 1″ apart.

Beat remaining egg in a small bowl. Brush tops of puffs with beaten egg and sprinkle with remaining Parmesan.

Place baking sheet on center rack and bake for 15-20 minutes until puffed and well browned. *Yield: approximately 20 puffs.*

5	OUNCES GOAT CHEESE CUT INTO 1-OUNCE SLICES
¼	CUP BRANDY
2	TABLESPOONS WALNUT OIL
12	CLOVES GARLIC, UNPEELED
1	POUND GROUND VEAL
1	POUND GROUND PORK
1	POUND GROUND FATBACK
½	CUP FINELY CHOPPED ONION
½	CUP WALNUT PIECES
4	TEASPOONS SALT
2	TEASPOONS FRESHLY GROUND BLACK PEPPER
2	TEASPOONS FRESH THYME
¼	TEASPOON GROUND CINNAMON
¼	TEASPOON GROUND CORIANDER
¼	TEASPOON GROUND CLOVES
1	PINCH GRATED NUTMEG
3	EGGS LIGHTLY BEATEN
2	BAY LEAVES

PÂTÉ WITH GOAT CHEESE

Preheat oven to 350° F. Place cheese in large nonaluminum bowl. Add brandy and oil and marinate 1 hour. Remove cheese from marinade. Set aside.

Drop garlic into pan of boiling water. Cook 3 minutes. Drain. Refresh. Drain again, peel and mince. Add to marinade.

In the bowl containing marinade, mix together remaining ingredients except for bay leaves and cheese. Tightly pack half the mixture into buttered 1½-quart terrine. Lay reserved cheese slices down the center. Cover with remaining meat mixture and pack firmly. Arrange bay leaves on top and cover with foil. Place terrine in roasting pan and add hot water to come halfway up sides. Bake for 1¼ hours.

Remove foil and bake ½ hour longer. Cool in water bath ½ hour. Cover terrine with foil and top with weights. Drain occasionally while cooling. Remove pâté from terrine and drain. Wrap in plastic wrap or cheesecloth and refrigerate 24 hours before serving. *Yield: 8 to 10 servings.*

1	TABLESPOON UNFLAVORED GELATIN
2½	CUPS CLEAR GREEN TURTLE SOUP
6	OUNCES CREAM CHEESE
2	TABLESPOONS WHIPPING CREAM
¼	TEASPOON MINCED GARLIC
½	TEASPOON BEAU MONDE SEASONING
½	CUP PÂTÉ DE FOIE GRAS

PÂTÉ MOLD EN GELÉE DE TORTUE

Soften gelatin in ¼ cup of the soup. Heat remaining soup to a boil and add gelatin mixture, stirring until dissolved.

Soften cream cheese with cream and blend in garlic and Beau Monde.

Pour ½ of the soup mixture into 4-cup ring mold and chill until it starts to gel.

Drop pâté by rounded spoonsful on top of gelled soup. Refrigerate. Spread cream cheese mixture over pâté. Pour remainder of the soup into mold and chill thoroughly.

Unmold pâté and serve with croutons. *Yield: 15 servings.*

2	TABLESPOONS BUTTER
16	SMALL MUSHROOM CAPS
1	TABLESPOON FRESHLY GRATED GINGER ROOT
1	POUND BAY SCALLOPS, DRAINED
⅔	CUP DRY WHITE WINE
1	TABLESPOON FRESHLY SQUEEZED LEMON JUICE
1	CUP WHIPPING CREAM
	SALT AND FRESHLY GROUND PEPPER
1½	TABLESPOONS FRESHLY GRATED PARMESAN CHEESE
	ITALIAN PARSLEY AS GARNISH

GINGERED SCALLOPS

Preheat broiler. Melt butter in large skillet. Add mushrooms and ginger. Sauté over medium heat for 1 minute. Add scallops and sauté 1 minute more. With a slotted spoon, transfer mushrooms and scallops to a platter and set aside.

Add wine and lemon juice to skillet, scraping up any brown particles. Cook until liquid is reduced by one-half. Blend in cream and continue cooking until mixture is again reduced by one-half.

Return scallops and mushrooms to skillet. Toss. Add salt and pepper to taste. Heat until warmed through and transfer to individual oven-proof serving dishes. Sprinkle with Parmesan cheese and broil until lightly browned.

Serve immediately, garnished with Italian parsley and a small flower or orchid. *Yield: 4 servings.*

2	POUNDS FRESH SPINACH, WASHED, STEMS REMOVED
3	EGGS
2	TABLESPOONS BUTTER
	FRESHLY GROUND PEPPER TO TASTE
	GRATED NUTMEG TO TASTE
	BECHAMEL SAUCE
1½	TABLESPOONS BUTTER
2	TABLESPOONS FLOUR
1	CUP MILK

SPINACH TIMBALES

For Bechamel Sauce, melt butter in saucepan over medium-low heat. Add flour and blend. Add milk slowly, stirring rapidly. Cook over low heat for 5 minutes until thickened. *Preheat oven to 325° F.*

Steam spinach over boiling water for 2 minutes. Transfer to food processor and process until puréed. Add eggs, butter, pepper, nutmeg and bechamel sauce. Process until smooth.

Butter individual timbales, molds or soufflé dishes. Fill the molds ⅔ full with spinach mixture. Place molds in a baking pan and fill pan with boiling water until water reaches halfway up sides of molds. Bake 20 minutes or until knife inserted in spinach comes out clean. *Yield: 6 servings.*

1	CUP SMALL MORELS
6	TABLESPOONS BUTTER
6	SMALL FLOUR TORTILLAS
6	SLICES MONTEREY JACK CHEESE

QUESADILLAS WITH MORELS

Sauté morels in butter until golden, about 5 minutes.

In a sauté pan heat tortillas, one at a time, turning with a spatula.

Place a slice of cheese on each tortilla, fold in half and continue to turn until cheese begins to melt. Top each cheese-filled tortilla with 3 tablespoons sautéed morels. Cut each tortilla in 3 pie-shaped sections and serve immediately. *Yield: 6 servings.*

1½	POUNDS FRESH SALMON FILETS
2	TABLESPOONS KOSHER SALT
1	TABLESPOON SUGAR
4	TABLESPOON FRESHLY SQUEEZED LIME JUICE
	BUTTER LETTUCE, BERMUDA ONION AND FRESH DILL AS GARNISH
	SWEET BLACK BREAD
	CAVIAR DRESSING
1½	TABLESPOONS FRESHLY SQUEEZED LEMON JUICE
¾	TEASPOON FRESHLY SQUEEZED LIME JUICE
1	TABLESPOON EXTRA VIRGIN OLIVE OIL
2	OUNCES BLACK CAVIAR

MARINATED SALMON WITH CAVIAR DRESSING

With boning knife, remove any remaining bones from filets. Scrape the skin side of the fish to remove any excess scales and score that side lightly.

Mix together salt and sugar. Rub into filets and place them in a shallow glass dish. Pour lime juice over. Marinate in refrigerator for 24 hours, turning filets 2 or 3 times.

For dressing, combine lemon and lime juices. Whisk in olive oil. Gently stir in caviar.

To serve, thinly slice salmon on a diagonal. Arrange several slices on a plate garnished with butter lettuce, thinly sliced Bermuda onion and sprigs of fresh dill. Serve with small slices of sweet black bread and caviar dressing on the side. *Yield: 8 to 10 servings.*

NOTE: Use extremely fresh filets, as the fish "cooks" in the lime juice.

2	TABLESPOONS EXTRA VIRGIN OLIVE OIL
1	ONION, CHOPPED
2	SMALL ZUCCHINI, SLICED
1	LARGE RED PEPPER, CUT INTO STRIPS
3	NEW POTATOES, PEELED, COOKED, SLICED
8	PITTED BLACK OLIVES, SLICED
8	EGGS
⅓	CUP MILK
½	TEASPOON SALT
¼	TEASPOON WHITE PEPPER
½	CUP FRESHLY GRATED PARMESAN CHEESE

VEGETABLE FRITTATA

In a large skillet heat olive oil and sauté onion for 5 minutes. Add zucchini and red pepper and sauté for 5 minutes or until soft. Stir in potatoes and olives. Cool. *Preheat oven to 350° F.*

In a bowl beat eggs with remaining ingredients.

Line a 9″ square baking pan with foil. Heavily butter bottom and sides of foil. Spoon in vegetables, spreading them in an even layer. Pour egg mixture evenly over vegetables. Bake for 35-40 minutes or until puffed and golden brown. Remove from heat and cool 10 minutes.

To serve warm, use foil to lift frittata from pan. Turn down sides of foil and cut into 2″ squares. To serve cold, chill frittata in pan, then remove and cut. Garnish top of each square as desired. *Yield: Sixteen 2″ squares.*

SUGGESTED GARNISHES: Asparagus tips and pimento strips; mushroom slices, white onion rings and parsley; small stuffed olives and parsley; pickle fan and black olive slices; cherry tomato slices topped with pumpkin seeds.

8	OUNCES WHIPPED BUTTER
16	OUNCES CREAM CHEESE, SOFTENED
2	CLOVES GARLIC, PRESSED
1	TEASPOON FRESH OREGANO
1	TEASPOON FRESH DILL WEED
½	TEASPOON FRESH BASIL
½	TEASPOON FRESH THYME
½	TEASPOON FRESH MARJORAM
¼	TEASPOON FRESHLY GROUND BLACK PEPPER

POTTED HERB CHEESE

Mix all ingredients together and refrigerate overnight to blend flavors.

Serve at room temperature in a crock along with your favorite crackers. *Yield: 3 cups.*

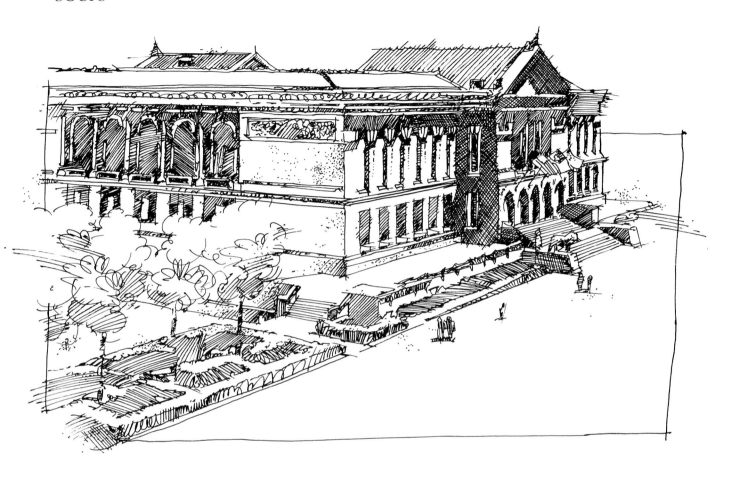

THE ART INSTITUTE OF CHICAGO is guarded by two large, sculptured lions. The Institute boasts a large collection of French Impressionist paintings as well as works by El Greco, Goya and Rembrandt. It is also home to significant collections of oriental, primitive and contemporary art. The original section of the building was constructed in 1892 in the French Renaissance style. Newer additions house art and drama schools and a theatre as well as the original trading room—designed by Adler and Sullivan—from the Chicago Stock Exchange Building. (The Chicago Stock Exchange Building stood on LaSalle Street, in the heart of Chicago's financial district, until 1972.)

2	BOILING POTATOES, PEELED AND QUARTERED
1	CUP COARSELY CHOPPED ONION
½	CUP CHOPPED CELERY
¼	CUP WATER
½	CUP BUTTER
1	TABLESPOON FLOUR
4	CUPS MILK
1¼	TEASPOONS SALT
½	TEASPOON FRESHLY GROUND PEPPER
⅛	TEASPOON GROUND MACE
3	DROPS HOT RED PEPPER SAUCE
1	TEASPOON WORCESTERSHIRE SAUCE
1	TABLESPOON FRESHLY SQUEEZED LEMON JUICE
2	CUPS HALF-AND-HALF
1	POUND BLUE CRAB MEAT
4	THIN STRIPS LEMON PEEL LEMON SLICES AS GARNISH
8	TEASPOONS DRY SHERRY PAPRIKA AS GARNISH

BLUE CRAB SOUP

Cook potatoes in boiling, salted water until tender, about 20 minutes. Mash potatoes until smooth, set aside.

In a food processor combine onion, celery and water. Process until very smooth.

Melt 1 tablespoon butter in a skillet. Stir in onion and celery mixture. Cook 5 minutes, stirring constantly. Set aside.

Melt 1 tablespoon butter in a large saucepan; stir in flour. Cook over low heat, stirring constantly until mixture is smooth and bubbly. Remove from heat and stir in 1 cup of the milk. Return to heat and bring to a boil, stirring constantly for 1 minute. Stir in salt, pepper, mace, red pepper sauce, onion and celery mixture, Worcestershire sauce and 1 cup of the milk.

Gradually add lemon juice, stirring constantly to prevent curdling. Stir in potatoes, half-and-half and remaining 2 cups milk.

Stir in crabmeat, remaining butter and the lemon peel. Simmer 10 minutes.

Serve garnished with lemon slices, sherry and paprika.
Yield: 8 servings.

6	CUPS BEEF BROTH
6	MEDIUM RED POTATOES, UNPEELED AND DICED
2	SHALLOTS, PEELED AND SLICED
8	SPRIGS PARSLEY, STEMS REMOVED
4	TEASPOONS DIJON MUSTARD
¼	TEASPOON CAYENNE PEPPER
1	CUP GRATED EMMENTALER CHEESE

POTATO SOUP WITH EMMENTALER CHEESE

In a saucepan bring broth, potatoes, shallots and parsley to a boil and cook for 8-9 minutes or until potatoes are tender.

Place broth, vegetables, mustard and cayenne in food processor and purée.

Ladle into bowls and sprinkle with cheese. Serve immediately.
Yield: 6 servings.

3	TABLESPOONS BUTTER
1	CUP CHOPPED ONION
½	TEASPOON MINCED GARLIC
1¾	POUNDS BROCCOLI, COARSELY CHOPPED
2	BOILING POTATOES, PEELED AND QUARTERED
7	CUPS CHICKEN BROTH FRESHLY GROUND PEPPER TO TASTE
3	CUPS LOW-FAT BUTTERMILK
½	TEASPOON NUTMEG
¼	TEASPOON CAYENNE PEPPER
½	CUP CHOPPED FRESH DILL

BROCCOLI BUTTERMILK SOUP WITH DILL

In a saucepan heat butter and add onion and garlic. Cook, stirring until onion is transparent. Blend in broccoli and potatoes, chicken broth and pepper. Bring to a boil, reduce heat and simmer 20 minutes or until vegetables are tender.

Ladle mixture into food processor and blend thoroughly.

Return soup to saucepan and add buttermilk, nutmeg and cayenne. Heat thoroughly and serve immediately sprinkled with chopped dill. *Yield: 8 to 12 servings.*

2	TABLESPOONS BUTTER
3	LARGE SHALLOTS, PEELED AND CHOPPED
8	CARROTS, PEELED AND THINLY SLICED
½	LARGE TART APPLE, PEELED, CORED AND DICED
½	LARGE BOILING POTATO, PEELED AND DICED
3	CUPS CHICKEN STOCK SALT AND FRESHLY GROUND PEPPER TO TASTE
¼	CUP CRÈME FRAÎCHE SPRIGS OF FRESH CHERVIL, DILL OR PARSLEY AS GARNISH

SHALLOT CARROT SOUP

In a saucepan melt butter over medium heat. Add shallots and cook 5 minutes or until tender. Add carrots, apple and potato and continue cooking 10 minutes. Add stock and cook 10-15 minutes more, until vegetables are tender.

Transfer mixture to a food processor and process until smooth. Return mixture to saucepan and season with salt and pepper to taste. Serve hot with dollop of crème fraîche and chervil, dill or parsley. *Yield: 4 to 6 servings.*

3	TABLESPOONS BUTTER
1	CUP CHOPPED ONION
1	CUP CHOPPED CELERY
¾	CUP SLICED CARROTS
2½	CUPS BROCCOLI FLORETS
1½	CUPS CHICKEN BROTH
3	CUPS MILK
1	CUP SHREDDED CHEDDAR CHEESE
6	SLICES FRENCH BREAD, TOASTED
12	THIN SLICES GOUDA CHEESE
6	SLICES BACON, COOKED, DRAINED, CRUMBLED

COUNTRY CHEESE SOUP

Melt the butter in a large saucepan. Add onion and celery. Sauté for 5 minutes. Add carrots, broccoli and the broth. Cover and bring to a boil. Reduce heat to simmer and cook vegetables until tender, about 15 minutes.

Add milk and shredded Cheddar and stir until melted.

Preheat broiler. Pour the soup into 1 large or 6 individual crocks. Place bread slices on top of soup; cover with 2 slices of Gouda cheese. Broil until cheese melts and is delicate brown, about 2 minutes.

Sprinkle with crumbled bacon and serve immediately.
Yield: 6 servings.

¼	CUP VEGETABLE OIL
2	CUPS CHOPPED ONION
3¾	CUPS CHOPPED TOMATOES
3⅔	CUPS SLICED MUSHROOMS
2	CUPS BROCCOLI FLORETS
2	CUPS SLICED ZUCCHINI
1	CUP CHOPPED GREEN BELL PEPPER
3	TABLESPOONS CHILI POWDER
½	TEASPOON GARLIC POWDER
⅛	TEASPOON FRESHLY GROUND PEPPER
¼	CUP WATER
2	TEASPOONS FLOUR
16	OUNCES RED KIDNEY BEANS, COOKED AND DRAINED
3	CUPS COOKED LONG-GRAIN WHITE OR BROWN RICE
6	TABLESPOONS SOUR CREAM
6	GREEN ONIONS, CHOPPED
1	CUP SHREDDED CHEDDAR CHEESE

VEGETARIAN CHILI

Heat oil in large saucepan over medium-high heat. Add onion and sauté until translucent and softened. Reduce heat to medium and add tomatoes, mushrooms, broccoli, zucchini, bell pepper, chili powder, garlic powder and pepper. Cover and simmer until vegetables are crisp-tender, about 10 minutes.

Gradually combine water and flour and stir into vegetable mixture. Add beans and cook mixture until thickened, stirring frequently, about 5 minutes.

Divide rice among bowls. Spoon chili over rice. Top with sour cream, green onions and cheese. Serve immediately.
Yield: 6 servings.

½   CUP CHOPPED ONION
1   CLOVE GARLIC, MINCED
1   CUP SLICED CARROTS
1   CUP SLICED CELERY
1   CUP CUBED BOILING POTATOES
3½   CUPS CHICKEN BROTH
2   CUPS WHOLE KERNEL CORN,
       COOKED AND DRAINED
¼   CUP BUTTER
¼   CUP FLOUR
2   CUPS MILK
1   TABLESPOON DIJON MUSTARD
       PEPPER AND PAPRIKA TO TASTE
2   CUPS SHREDDED SHARP
       CHEDDAR CHEESE

CHEESY VEGETABLE CHOWDER

Combine onion, garlic, carrots, celery, potatoes and broth in large saucepan. Bring to a boil. Cover and reduce heat to simmer for 15-20 minutes until potatoes are tender. Stir in corn and remove from heat.

Melt butter in a heavy saucepan over low heat. Add flour, stirring until smooth. Cook 1 minute, stirring constantly. Remove from heat. Gradually whisk in milk. Return to medium heat and cook, stirring constantly until thick and bubbly. Add mustard, pepper, paprika and Cheddar, stirring constantly until cheese melts.

Gradually add cheese sauce to vegetable mixture. Stir until thoroughly heated. *Yield: 6 servings.*

1   TABLESPOON EXTRA VIRGIN
       OLIVE OIL
1   TABLESPOON BUTTER
1   CUP CHOPPED ONION
1   POUND GROUND ROUND STEAK
3   MEDIUM CARROTS, CHOPPED
3   STALKS CELERY, CHOPPED
28   OUNCES PLUM TOMATOES,
       INCLUDING LIQUID
1   EGGPLANT, PEELED AND DICED
2   CLOVES GARLIC, MINCED
28   OUNCES BEEF BROTH
1   TEASPOON SALT
½   TEASPOON SUGAR
½   TEASPOON NUTMEG
¾   CUP UNCOOKED ROTINI PASTA
       PARMESAN CHEESE,
         FRESHLY GRATED

EGGPLANT SOUP

In a large saucepan heat oil and butter. Cook onion until soft. Add ground round and brown. Drain fat. Add carrots and celery. Cook 2-3 minutes.

Add tomatoes, eggplant, garlic, broth, salt, sugar and nutmeg. Bring to a boil. Cover and reduce heat. Simmer 1½ hours, stirring occasionally.

Add pasta. Cover and simmer 15-20 minutes or until pasta is tender.

Serve immediately with Parmesan cheese. *Yield: 8 servings.*

2	POUNDS HADDOCK OR COD
2	CUPS PEELED AND DICED NEW POTATOES
¼	CUP CHOPPED CELERY LEAVES
3	BAY LEAVES
2½	TEASPOONS SALT
¼	TEASPOON WHITE PEPPER
4	WHOLE CLOVES
1	CLOVE GARLIC, MINCED
½	CUP BUTTER, MELTED
1	CUP DRY VERMOUTH
2	CUPS FISH STOCK, BOILING
2	CUPS HALF-AND-HALF
1½	TEASPOONS CHOPPED FRESH DILL AS GARNISH

CHICAGO FISH CHOWDER

Preheat oven to 350° F. In a large casserole combine all ingredients except fish stock, half-and-half and dill. Pour the boiling fish stock over all. Cover and bake for 50-60 minutes, until fish flakes and potatoes are tender.

In a small saucepan heat, but do not boil, the half-and-half. Add it to the chowder. Sprinkle dill on top and serve immediately. *Yield: 6 servings.*

1	CUP CHOPPED ONION
½	CUP BUTTER
4	CUPS CUCUMBER, PEELED, SEEDED AND CHOPPED
4	CUPS TOMATOES, PEELED, SEEDED AND CHOPPED
4	TABLESPOONS FLOUR
4	CUPS CHICKEN BROTH
½	CUP WHIPPING CREAM
	SALT AND FRESHLY GROUND PEPPER TO TASTE
	CHOPPED FRESH OREGANO OR BASIL AS GARNISH

CUCUMBER TOMATO SOUP

In a large skillet sauté onion in butter until transparent.

In a food processor blend onion, cucumbers, tomatoes, flour and broth until smooth.

Return mixture to skillet. Stir and heat until warm. Allow to cool. Add cream, salt and pepper and stir well. Chill.

Sprinkle with chopped fresh oregano or basil. *Yield: 6 servings.*

3	MEDIUM GRANNY SMITH APPLES, PEELED AND CORED
3	CUPS PURÉE OF COOKED BUTTERNUT SQUASH
3	CUPS CHICKEN STOCK
1	CUP WHIPPING CREAM OR CRÈME FRAÎCHE
2	TABLESPOONS BRANDY

WINTER SQUASH SOUP

In a food processor purée apples. Add squash and process until combined. Pour mixture into a large saucepan.

Add remaining ingredients and mix together.

Heat to simmer; do not let soup boil. Serve immediately.
Yield: 8 servings.

½	CUP BACON DRIPPINGS
1½	CUPS FLOUR
1½	CUPS CHOPPED ONIONS
½	CUP CHOPPED BELL PEPPER
1	CLOVE GARLIC, CHOPPED
½	TABLESPOON CELERY SEED
½	CUP CHOPPED FRESH PARSLEY
½	CUP SLICED GREEN ONION
	WATER
1	CUP SHUCKED AND CLEANED OYSTERS
½	POUND SHELLED SHRIMP
1	POUND SMOKED TURKEY, CUT UP
½	POUND ANDOUILLE OR SMOKED SAUSAGE
1	TEASPOON MINT
8	OUNCES COOKED RED BEANS, PURÉED WITH LIQUID
2	CUPS DRY, WHITE WINE
3	DROPS BITTERS
1	TABLESPOON HOT RED PEPPER SAUCE
2	TABLESPOONS WORCESTERSHIRE SAUCE
3	CUPS SLICED OKRA
	SALT AND FRESHLY GROUND PEPPER

SOON-TO-BE-FAMOUS GUMBO

In a large saucepan heat bacon drippings. Add flour and stir to make a roux. Cook over low heat until dark brown.

Add onions, bell pepper, garlic and celery seed. Cook until onions are soft. Add parsley and green onions and cook briefly.

Add 3 tablespoons water and stir to make a thick paste.

Add remaining ingredients and cover with 3 inches of water. Bring to a boil, reduce heat, cover and simmer 3-4 hours.

Remove from heat, add salt and pepper to taste and serve immediately. *Yield: 8 to 10 servings.*

½ CUP CHOPPED LEEKS, WHITE
PART ONLY
4 TABLESPOONS UNSALTED
BUTTER
½ POUND DOMESTIC
MUSHROOMS, THINLY SLICED
½ POUND FRESH SHIITAKE,
CHANTERELLE OR PORCINI
MUSHROOMS, THINLY SLICED
⅓ CUP DRIED WILD MUSHROOMS,
SOFTENED IN ½ CUP
WARM WHITE WINE
4 LARGE BOILING POTATOES,
PEELED AND THINLY SLICED
1 QUART CHICKEN STOCK
1½ CUPS HALF-AND-HALF
1 CUP WHIPPING CREAM
SALT, FRESHLY GROUND PEPPER
AND NUTMEG TO TASTE
WHIPPED CREAM AND 6
SAUTÉED MUSHROOM CAPS
AS GARNISH

MANY MUSHROOM SOUP

In a saucepan cook leeks in butter until tender. Add all mushrooms and wine and cook until softened. Add potatoes and stock and simmer, covered, until potatoes are very soft, about 30 minutes. Cool slightly.

Purée cooled mixture in a food processor. Return mixture to saucepan. Add half-and-half, cream and seasonings and heat through. Do not boil.

Ladle into bowls and garnish each serving with a dollop of whipped cream and a mushroom cap. *Yield: 6 servings.*

20 OUNCES FRESH
SPINACH, CHOPPED
4 THIN SLICES WHITE
ONION, CHOPPED
½ CUP WATER
6 CUPS CHICKEN BROTH
4 TABLESPOONS BUTTER
2 TABLESPOONS FLOUR
SALT AND FRESHLY
GROUND PEPPER
2 CUPS HALF-AND-HALF
1 CUP FRESH CRABMEAT
½ TEASPOON NUTMEG

SPINACH SOUP WITH CRABMEAT

Steam spinach and onion in water until tender.

Place spinach and 2 cups of the broth in food processor or blender and purée.

In a saucepan melt butter. Stir in flour, salt and pepper to taste. Remove from heat. Gradually whisk in remaining 4 cups of broth, return to heat and bring to a boil. Add puréed spinach and onion and simmer for 20 minutes. Add half-and-half.

Immediately before serving add crabmeat. Serve sprinkled with nutmeg. *Yield: 10 to 12 servings.*

4	LARGE ONIONS, SLICED THINLY
5	TABLESPOONS UNSALTED BUTTER
3	TABLESPOONS FLOUR
6	CUPS CHICKEN STOCK
½	TEASPOON TURMERIC
	SALT AND FRESHLY GROUND PEPPER TO TASTE
⅓	CUP SUGAR
¼	CUP FRESHLY SQUEEZED LIME JUICE
¼	TEASPOON CINNAMON
¼	TEASPOON GROUND CARDAMOM
2	TABLESPOONS MINCED FRESH MINT LEAVES
2	EGGS

PERSIAN MINTED ONION SOUP

In a large saucepan cook onions in butter over moderate heat, stirring occasionally, until they are golden. Sprinkle the mixture with flour and cook over moderately low heat, stirring for 2 minutes.

Add the stock in a stream, stirring constantly. Add the turmeric and salt and pepper to taste. Bring the liquid to a boil and simmer, covered, for 40 minutes. Stir in sugar and lime juice. Simmer for 10 minutes and add cinnamon, cardamom, and 1 tablespoon of the mint. Remove from heat.

In a small bowl lightly beat the eggs. Whisk in ½ cup of the hot liquid. Add this mixture in a stream to the saucepan, stirring to combine.

Ladle the soup into bowls and serve garnished with remaining fresh mint. *Yield: 6 servings.*

4	TABLESPOONS BUTTER
1	CUP CELERY, SLICED DIAGONALLY
1	CUP SCALLIONS, SLICED DIAGONALLY
48	OUNCES CHICKEN BROTH
1	CUP LEAF LETTUCE, ROLLED AND SHREDDED
1	CUP FRESH SORREL LEAVES, ROLLED AND SLICED THIN
	SALT AND FRESHLY GROUND PEPPER
	PARMESAN CHEESE
	CROUTONS

SOUP VERTE

Melt butter in large saucepan. Add celery and scallions and cook gently until transparent. Add chicken broth. Heat thoroughly. Add lettuce and sorrel, cooking just to soften. Season with salt and pepper to taste.

Serve immediately with Parmesan cheese and croutons. *Yield: 6 to 8 servings.*

4 TABLESPOONS BUTTER
⅓ CUP CHOPPED GREEN ONIONS
1 STALK CELERY,
    COARSELY CHOPPED
1½ CUPS SHELLED, FRESH PEAS
1¾ CUPS CHICKEN BROTH
6 FRESH MINT LEAVES, CHOPPED
    SALT AND FRESHLY GROUND
    PEPPER TO TASTE
1 LARGE RIPE AVOCADO, PEELED
    AND PITTED
2 TEASPOONS FRESHLY SQUEEZED
    LEMON JUICE
1 CUP HALF-AND-HALF
    MINT SPRIGS AS GARNISH
1 LARGE RIPE AVOCADO, PEELED,
    PITTED, SLICED INTO
    THIN SLIVERS

SPRING MINT, PEA AND AVOCADO SOUP

Melt butter in large saucepan over low heat. Add onions, celery, peas and broth. Bring to a boil; reduce heat to low. Cover. Simmer until vegetables are tender, about 20 minutes.

Add mint, salt and pepper. Simmer, uncovered, about 5 minutes, just to blend flavors.

Strain soup over large bowl, reserving broth. Put vegetables, avocado and lemon juice into food processor and process until smooth. Add some of the reserved broth to thin.

Return puréed vegetables, remaining broth and half-and-half to saucepan. Cook, stirring constantly until heated through. Correct seasonings. Serve hot or cold.

Garnish each serving with sprigs of fresh mint and a sliver of avocado. *Yield: 4 to 6 servings.*

3½ CUPS CHICKEN BROTH
¼ CUP LONG-GRAIN WHITE RICE
1½ CUPS COARSELY
    CHOPPED BROCCOLI
1 CUP CHOPPED CARROTS
3 TABLESPOONS FLOUR
1 TEASPOON CURRY POWDER
1½ CUPS MILK
    SALT AND FRESHLY GROUND
    PEPPER TO TASTE

CURRIED VEGETABLE CHOWDER

In a large saucepan stir together chicken broth and rice. Bring to a boil and reduce heat. Cover and simmer for 10 minutes. Stir in broccoli and carrots. Return to a boil. Reduce heat to simmer, and cook for 10 minutes or until vegetables and rice are tender.

In a small bowl combine flour and curry powder. Gradually whisk in the milk. Add to vegetable and rice mixture. Cook and stir until thick and bubbly. Cook 1 minute more.

Season soup to taste with salt and pepper. *Yield: 4 to 6 servings.*

2	QUARTS CHICKEN BROTH
	COARSE SALT TO TASTE
4	EGGS
½	CUP FRESHLY SQUEEZED
	LEMON JUICE
2	SMALL ZUCCHINI
½	CUP ORZO PASTA
	EXTRA VIRGIN OLIVE OIL
1	LEMON, THINLY SLICED

LEMON-ZUCCHINI SOUP

Heat chicken broth to a boil in a large, nonaluminum saucepan. Add salt to taste. Set aside.

Beat eggs in medium bowl until thick and frothy. Slowly add lemon juice, whisking constantly. Slowly add 2 cups of hot broth, whisking constantly to prevent eggs from curdling. Stir egg and lemon mixture into remainder of broth. Let cool and chill.

In a food processor julienne zucchini into strips. Cook in boiling salted water for 45 seconds just to set the color and remove the raw taste. Drain quickly and run under cold water to cool. Chill.

Cook orzo in boiling salted water until al dente, about 10 minutes. Drain. Run under cold water until cool. Drain again and set aside. (If preparing orzo more than half an hour ahead, place in a bowl and add 1 teaspoon olive oil to prevent sticking.) Chill.

Mix zucchini and orzo with soup. Adjust seasonings. Serve chilled, garnished with lemon slices. *Yield: 6 servings.*

½	CUP BUTTER
1	CUP CHOPPED ONION
2½	CUPS CHICKEN STOCK
1½	POUNDS SHREDDED ZUCCHINI
2	TEASPOONS FRESHLY
	GRATED NUTMEG
2	TEASPOONS FRESH BASIL
	SALT AND WHITE PEPPER
	TO TASTE
	CRUMBLED BACON AS GARNISH

ZUCCHINI BISQUE

In a large saucepan, over medium heat, melt butter. Add onion and cook until tender.

Add stock, zucchini, nutmeg and basil. Heat until mixture boils. Reduce heat and cover. Simmer 15 minutes.

Transfer to food processor and purée until smooth. Salt and pepper to taste.

Serve hot or cold garnished with bacon. *Yield: 4 servings.*

NOTE: This soup does not have a cream base, which makes it a uniquely delicious zucchini soup.

THE AUDITORIUM BUILDING was designed by architects Dankmar Adler and Louis Sullivan. When it opened in 1889 the great lobby and grand staircase were the showpieces of the building. The original building included the Auditorium Theatre, a hotel and office space. The Auditorium Theatre, known for its large stage and perfect acoustics, was restored in 1946 and is still used for productions. The rest of the building was purchased by Roosevelt University that same year and currently serves as part of its downtown campus.

2 CUPS FLOUR
1½ CUPS SUGAR
2 TEASPOONS BAKING POWDER
¼ TEASPOON SALT
⅔ CUP UNSALTED
   BUTTER, SOFTENED
2 EGGS
¾ CUP MILK
1 TEASPOON VANILLA EXTRACT
½ TEASPOON ALMOND EXTRACT
½ CUP CHOPPED ALMONDS
¾ TEASPOON CINNAMON
¼ TEASPOON ALLSPICE

ALMOND CRUMB BREAD

Preheat oven to 350° F. Grease a 9″ x 5″ loaf pan. Line the bottom and long sides of pan with waxed paper and allow a 3″ overhang of paper at the top.

Sift flour, sugar, baking powder and salt into a large bowl. Cut in butter until mixture resembles coarse meal. Remove ½ cup of flour mixture to a medium bowl and set aside.

Stir eggs, milk, vanilla and almond extracts into original flour mixture and beat until blended. Pour about 1 cup of the batter into prepared pan.

Add almond, cinnamon and allspice to reserved flour mixture and stir well.

Sprinkle ⅓ of the nut mixture over the batter in the pan. Repeat layering twice, ending with nut mixture.

Bake until a toothpick inserted in center is withdrawn clean, about 70-80 minutes. Loosen sides of loaf from pan with wide spatula. Grasping waxed paper firmly, pull loaf from pan. Cool on wire rack. *Yield: 1 loaf.*

½ CUP BUTTER
3 OUNCES CREAM
   CHEESE, SOFTENED
1 CUP FIRMLY PACKED
   BROWN SUGAR
2 RIPE BANANAS, MASHED
1 EGG
¼ CUP SOUR CREAM
1½ CUPS FLOUR
¾ CUP CHOCOLATE CHIPS
1 TEASPOON BAKING SODA
1 TEASPOON BAKING POWDER
½ TEASPOON SALT

BANANA CREAM CHOCOLATE CHIP MUFFINS

Preheat oven to 325° F. In a bowl cream together butter, cream cheese and brown sugar. Add bananas, egg and sour cream. Mix thoroughly.

In a large bowl combine remaining ingredients and make a well. Pour wet ingredients into well and mix.

Fill greased muffin tins ⅔ full. Bake for 20 to 25 minutes. *Yield: 1 dozen muffins.*

2	CUPS FLOUR
½	TEASPOON SALT
2½	TEASPOONS BAKING POWDER
¼	CUP CONFECTIONER'S SUGAR
6	TABLESPOONS COLD BUTTER, CUT INTO ¼″ PIECES
1	EGG
	MILK
¾	CUP FRESH BLUEBERRIES

BLUEBERRY SCONES

In a medium bowl combine flour, salt, baking powder and sugar.

Cut the butter into the dry ingredients until mixture has texture of coarse meal.

Lightly beat egg in measuring cup and add enough milk to total ⅔ cup liquid. Add egg mixture to dry mixture and gently stir with a fork until mixture holds together. Fold in blueberries.

Preheat oven to 425° F. Gather dough into a ball and place on a lightly floured board. Knead gently, 10-12 strokes, adding flour to board as necessary. Pat dough into a square ½″ thick. Cut into 4 squares, then cut each square into 4 triangles.

Place scones on ungreased baking sheet about 1″ apart and bake 12 minutes.

Serve with crème fraîche or clotted cream. *Yield: 16 scones.*

1	CUP FLOUR
1	CUP WHOLE WHEAT FLOUR
⅔	CUP FIRMLY PACKED BROWN SUGAR
¼	CUP WHOLE BRAN CEREAL
1	TEASPOON BAKING SODA
1	TEASPOON CINNAMON
¼	TEASPOON SALT
1	EGG, BEATEN
6	OUNCES YOGURT WITH FRUITS, RAISINS AND GRAINS
¼	CUP MILK
¼	CUP VEGETABLE OIL

BREAKFAST YOGURT BREAD

Preheat oven to 350° F. In a medium bowl combine both flours, sugar, cereal, baking soda, cinnamon and salt. Make a well in the center. Set aside.

In a small bowl combine egg, yogurt, milk and oil. Add yogurt mixture to the flour mixture. Stir just until moistened.

Pour into a greased 8″ x 4″ loaf pan. Bake about 50 minutes or until a toothpick inserted near the center comes out clean. Cool in pan for 10 minutes. Remove bread from pan.

Serve warm or at room temperature. *Yield: 1 loaf.*

CAMEMBERT FRENCH BREAD

4	OUNCES CAMEMBERT CHEESE
½	TEASPOON FINELY MINCED FRESH BASIL
½	CUP BUTTER
½	TEASPOON ONION SALT
1	LARGE LOAF FRENCH BREAD

Preheat oven to 325° F. In a saucepan combine cheese, basil, butter and salt and simmer 5 minutes, stirring constantly, until blended.

Remove from heat and cool 10 minutes or until mixture starts to thicken.

Slice bread in half lengthwise and spread ⅓ of cheese mixture on each half. Put halves together and spread remaining cheese mixture on top.

Wrap bread in aluminum foil and bake for 15 minutes. Turn back foil to brown bread for another 5 minutes. *Yield: 1 large loaf.*

CARAWAY CHEESE MUFFINS

¾	CUP FLOUR
1	CUP RYE FLOUR
¼	CUP SUGAR
2½	TEASPOONS BAKING POWDER
½	TEASPOON SALT
1	EGG, BEATEN
¾	CUP MILK
⅓	CUP VEGETABLE OIL
¾	CUP SHREDDED CHEDDAR CHEESE
1½	TEASPOONS CARAWAY SEEDS

Preheat oven to 400° F. Grease a 12-cup muffin tin. In a large bowl stir together the flours, sugar, baking powder and salt. Make a well in the center.

In another bowl combine the egg, milk and oil. Add egg mixture to the flour mixture. Stir just until moistened.

Combine cheese and caraway seeds; fold into batter.

Fill muffin cups ⅔ full. Bake for 20-25 minutes or until golden brown. Serve warm. *Yield: 12 muffins.*

FRECKLED PEPPER CHEESE BREAD

3	OUNCES SWISS CHEESE
3	OUNCES PARMESAN CHEESE
¼	CUP EXTRA VIRGIN OLIVE OIL
2	TEASPOONS DIJON MUSTARD
1½	TEASPOONS COARSELY CRACKED BLACK PEPPER
1	LOAF FRENCH BREAD

Preheat oven to 350° F. Mince cheeses in a food processor. Add oil, mustard and pepper and process to a paste.

Make diagonal slits at 1″ intervals in bread, cutting from top, almost to the bottom. Do not cut through bottom crust. Carefully open bread at slits and spread with cheese mixture. Wrap bread in foil.

Bake on center rack until cheese is melted, about 30 minutes. Serve hot. *Yield: 8 servings.*

FRENCH TOAST WITH BRANDIED LEMON BUTTER

4	EGGS
2	TABLESPOONS PLUS 1 TEASPOON SUGAR
½	TEASPOON SALT
1	CUP MILK
¼	TEASPOON VANILLA EXTRACT
12	SLICES DRY BREAD
	BUTTER
	LEMON SLICES
	CONFECTIONER'S SUGAR
	BRANDIED LEMON BUTTER
½	CUP CLARIFIED BUTTER
1	CUP SUGAR
	JUICE OF 2 LEMONS
4	TEASPOONS GRATED LEMON RIND
3	OUNCES BRANDY OR RUM

For Brandied Lemon Butter, in a saucepan, over low heat, combine clarified butter and sugar. Stir continuously until sugar dissolves. Add lemon juice, rind and brandy. Stir until smooth. Set aside.

In a shallow dish beat eggs, sugar, salt, milk and vanilla.

Soak bread in the mixture.

Heat butter over medium-high heat and cook each slice of bread until slightly brown on each side. Serve with Brandied Lemon Butter and lemon slices. Sprinkle with confectioner's sugar. *Yield: 6 servings.*

¾ CUP FLOUR
2 TABLESPOONS SUGAR
1 TEASPOON BAKING POWDER
  PINCH OF SALT
1 EGG, BEATEN
⅓ CUP MILK
2 TABLESPOONS BUTTER, MELTED
  AND COOLED
½ TEASPOON ALMOND EXTRACT
1 PEACH, PEELED, PITTED
  AND DICED
¼ CUP CHOPPED ALMONDS

MINI PEACH MUFFINS

Preheat oven to 400° F. In a bowl combine flour, sugar, baking powder and salt.

In a separate bowl combine egg, milk, butter and extract. Add liquid ingredients to dry ingredients and stir just until combined.

Gently fold in peaches and almonds just until combined.

Spoon into buttered mini muffin tins and bake 15 to 20 minutes. *Yield: 16 mini muffins.*

¾ CUP SUGAR
2 CUPS FLOUR
¼ CUP MILLER'S BRAN
¼ CUP ROLLED OATS
2 TABLESPOONS WHEAT GERM
2 TEASPOONS GROUND
  CINNAMON
2 TEASPOONS BAKING SODA
  PINCH OF SALT
¾ CUP FLAKED, UNSWEETENED
  COCONUT
1 CUP DARK RAISINS
2 CUPS GRATED CARROTS
1 APPLE, GRATED
¾ CHOPPED WALNUTS
3 EGGS, BEATEN
1 CUP VEGETABLE OIL
1½ TEASPOONS VANILLA EXTRACT
  SUGAR

MORNING GLORY MUFFINS

Preheat oven to 375° F. In a large bowl combine sugar, flour, bran, oats, wheat germ, cinnamon, baking soda and salt. Set aside.

In a small bowl mix coconut, raisins, carrots, apple and nuts. Add to dry ingredients.

In a small bowl beat together eggs, oil and vanilla. Add to dry mixture and stir just until blended. Do not overmix.

Fill greased muffin tins ¾ full. Sprinkle tops with sugar to create a glaze.

Bake for 20 minutes. *Yield: 18 to 20 muffins.*

2	CUPS FLOUR
2	TABLESPOONS SUGAR
3	TEASPOONS BAKING POWDER
	PINCH OF SALT
⅓	CUP LIGHTLY SALTED BUTTER
1	EGG, BEATEN
½	CUP MILK
½	CUP CURRANTS
1	EGG LIGHTLY BEATEN WITH 1
	TABLESPOON MILK, AS GLAZE

MINI SCONES WITH CURRANTS

Preheat oven to 425° F. In a large bowl combine flour, sugar, baking powder and salt. Cut in butter until mixture resembles coarse meal. Gently fold in egg and milk just until combined. Do not stir. Fold in currants.

Drop batter by level tablespoons onto buttered baking sheet. Brush tops of scones with egg glaze and bake for 10-12 minutes, or until golden brown. *Yield: 40 mini scones.*

½	CUP BUTTER, SOFTENED
2	EGGS, BEATEN
¾	TEASPOON SALT
1	TEASPOON BAKING POWDER
1½	CUPS FLOUR
1¼	CUPS SUGAR
	GRATED RIND OF 1 LEMON
	JUICE OF 1 LEMON
	GLAZE
¼	CUP CONFECTIONER'S SUGAR
	GRATED RIND OF 1 LEMON
	JUICE OF 1 LEMON

LEMON TEA BREAD

Preheat oven to 350° F. In a large bowl combine all ingredients except glaze. Beat until thoroughly mixed.

Spoon batter into a greased 9″ x 5″ x 3″ loaf pan. Bake for 1 hour, or until a toothpick inserted in center comes out clean. Remove bread from pan.

In a small bowl combine all glaze ingredients. Beat until thoroughly mixed. Spread glaze over warm loaf.

Chill bread until ready to serve. *Yield: 1 loaf.*

3	CUPS FLOUR, SIFTED
1	TEASPOON BAKING SODA
1	TEASPOON SALT
2	TEASPOONS CINNAMON
2	CUPS SUGAR
4	EGGS, BEATEN
1½	CUPS VEGETABLE OIL
1	CUP CHOPPED PECANS
1½	PINTS FRESH STRAWBERRIES

STRAWBERRY BREAD

Preheat oven to 350° F. In a bowl combine flour, soda, salt, cinnamon and sugar and mix well.

Mix eggs and oil and add to dry ingredients. Stir in pecans. Fold in strawberries until moistened.

Pour into two greased 9″ x 5″ loaf pans and bake for 50-60 minutes or until toothpick inserted in center comes out clean. *Yield: 2 loaves*

1	LOAF SOFT WHITE BREAD
12	OUNCES SMOOTH PEANUT BUTTER
¾	CUP VEGETABLE OIL
1	TEASPOON SUGAR

PEANUT BUTTER STICKS

Preheat oven to 275° F. Remove bread crusts and reserve. Cut each slice in half, then in thirds (to finger size).

Place bread strips on ungreased baking sheet. Place reserved crusts on another baking sheet. Dry strips and crusts in oven for 45 minutes.

Remove bread from oven and process crusts into crumbs.

In a double boiler melt peanut butter, oil and sugar. Dip toasted bread strips in hot mixture and roll in crumbs. Drain on paper towels.

Cool and serve. *Yield: 3 dozen.*

2	PACKAGES ACTIVE DRY YEAST
3	TABLESPOONS SUGAR
2	TEASPOONS SALT
4	CUPS FLOUR, SIFTED
1½	CUPS LOW-FAT MILK
1	TABLESPOON UNSALTED BUTTER
½	CUP SHREDDED SWISS CHEESE
½	CUP SHREDDED CHEDDAR CHEESE
½	CUP FRESHLY GRATED PARMESAN CHEESE

THREE CHEESE BREAD

In a large bowl mix yeast, sugar and salt with 2 cups of the flour. Set aside.

Heat milk and butter to 110° F. Slowly beat this mixture into the dry ingredients. Blend well and continue beating for 1 to 2 minutes. Slowly stir in the three cheeses and the remaining flour until the batter is stiff. Cover bowl, set in a warm place and allow to rise until doubled in size, about 1 hour.

Preheat oven to 350° F. Punch down the batter and place it into a well-greased 9″ loaf pan. Bake for 45 minutes. Lay a piece of foil on the top (do not seal) and bake for another 15 minutes. The bread is done if it sounds hollow when tapped with the flat side of a knife blade. Remove the bread immediately and cool on a rack. *Yield: 1 loaf.*

TOASTED TOMATO BREAD

6	SLICES ITALIAN BREAD, ¾″ THICK
1	GARLIC CLOVE
½	POUND RIPE TOMATOES, CHOPPED
½	CUP CHOPPED RED ONION
8	FRESH BASIL LEAVES, CHOPPED
	DRIED OREGANO
	SALT AND FRESHLY GROUND PEPPER
	EXTRA VIRGIN OLIVE OIL

Preheat oven to 350° F. Toast bread on both sides. Rub one side of toast with fresh garlic clove.

Mix together tomatoes, onion and basil. Spread tomato mixture on garlic side of bread. Sprinkle with oregano, salt, pepper and oil.

Bake 10 minutes. *Yield: 6 servings.*

WALNUT WHEAT BREAD

1	CUP WATER, 100-110° F.
¼	CUP FIRMLY PACKED BROWN SUGAR
1	TABLESPOON DRY YEAST
1	EGG, SLIGHTLY BEATEN
1	TEASPOON SALT
3	TABLESPOONS WALNUT OIL
½	CUP WHOLE WHEAT FLOUR
3½	CUPS FLOUR
1½	CUPS CHOPPED WALNUTS
1	EGG, BEATEN
1	TEASPOON SALT

In a large bowl combine water, brown sugar and yeast to dissolve.

Mix together egg, salt and oil. Add to yeast mixture.

Add whole wheat flour and half of the white flour to the mixture. Beat well. Add walnuts, another cup of flour and mix well. Add remaining flour, a little at a time, mixing until a good consistency is achieved.

Remove dough from bowl. Knead well on a lightly-floured surface. Place in lightly greased bowl. Cover with a towel and let rise in a warm place until doubled, approximately 1 hour. Punch down and let rise a second time, 30-45 minutes.

Divide bread into 6 small loaf pans (6″ x 3″). Shape and let rise until doubled.

Preheat oven to 375° F. Glaze with mixture of beaten egg and salt.

Bake for 16-20 minutes until golden brown.

Yield: 6 small loaves.

RICHARD J. DALEY PLAZA is the site of a sculpture given to the city of
Chicago by Pablo Picasso. Made of Cor-Ten steel (identical to that
used in the Daley Center building), this powerful piece of work
benefits from its setting. Visitors can walk completely around the
sculpture, viewing it from all angles and vantage points. The
original model for the sculpture is housed in the Art Institute
of Chicago. The Picasso sculpture has prompted a great deal
of discussion among Chicagoans and visitors alike.

1 LARGE BUNCH ARUGULA,
    CLEANED AND STEMMED
1 HEAD RADICCHIO,
    STEMS REMOVED
1 BUNCH MUSTARD SPROUTS,
    ROOTS REMOVED
    MUSTARD VINAIGRETTE
4 TABLESPOONS EXTRA VIRGIN
    OLIVE OIL
1½ TABLESPOONS RED
    WINE VINEGAR
1½ TEASPOONS DIJON MUSTARD
    SALT AND FRESHLY GROUND
    PEPPER TO TASTE

ARUGULA, RADICCHIO AND MUSTARD SPROUT SALAD

For vinaigrette, whisk all ingredients together until smooth.

Toss salad ingredients together with mustard vinaigrette and serve. *Yield: 4 to 6 servings.*

½ POUND ARUGULA, CLEANED
    AND STEMMED
2 RIPE PLUM TOMATOES, SLICED
16-20 NIÇOISE OLIVES
⅓ CUP TOASTED PINE NUTS
    CONFETTI DRESSING
1 HARD-COOKED EGG, WHITE
    ONLY, FINELY CHOPPED
2 TABLESPOONS FINELY CHOPPED
    GREEN OLIVES
2 TABLESPOONS FINELY CHOPPED
    RED ONION
6 TABLESPOONS FINELY CHOPPED
    YELLOW BELL PEPPER
½ TEASPOON FINELY
    CHOPPED GARLIC
1 TABLESPOON FINELY
    CHOPPED PARSLEY
½ CUP RED WINE VINEGAR
1½ CUPS EXTRA VIRGIN OLIVE OIL
½ TEASPOON SALT
⅛ TEASPOON FRESHLY
    GROUND PEPPER

ARUGULA AND PINE NUT SALAD WITH CONFETTI DRESSING

For dressing combine the egg, green olives, onion, pepper, garlic and parsley in a bowl. Add vinegar and then olive oil in a steady stream, stirring constantly. Season with salt and pepper. Cover. Let sit at room temperature for 2½ hours.

Divide arugula among 4 salad plates. Arrange tomato slices and olives on the arugula. Stir dressing and spoon over the salads. Top with pine nuts. *Yield: 4 servings.*

4	CUPS BROCCOLI FLORETS
6	SCALLIONS, THINLY SLICED
4	OUNCES WATER CHESTNUTS, SLICED
5	OUNCES BLUE CHEESE, CRUMBLED
	LEAF LETTUCE
¼	CUP TOASTED PINE NUTS
	VINAIGRETTE DRESSING
⅓	CUP RED WINE VINEGAR
½	CUP EXTRA VIRGIN OLIVE OIL
1	CLOVE GARLIC, MINCED
½	TEASPOON SALT
	FRESHLY GROUND PEPPER

BROCCOLI BLUE CHEESE SALAD

Place broccoli in large saucepan. Pour boiling water over and let stand 2 minutes. Drain and immediately refresh with cold water. Drain again. Chill.

For dressing, combine all ingredients in a container with a tightly fitting lid and shake well.

Toss broccoli with scallions, chestnuts, blue cheese and dressing. Serve on a bed of lettuce, garnished with pine nuts. *Yield: 8 servings.*

1	MEDIUM BUNCH FRESH BROCCOLI
½	CUP EXTRA VIRGIN OLIVE OIL
3	TABLESPOONS RED WINE VINEGAR
½	TEASPOON SALT
	FRESHLY GROUND PEPPER
1	TEASPOON CHOPPED FRESH BASIL
1	TEASPOON DRY MUSTARD
1	CLOVE GARLIC, CRUSHED
⅓	CUP MAYONNAISE
1½	TABLESPOONS SOUR CREAM
1	TABLESPOON DICED PIMENTOS
1	TABLESPOON CAPERS, DRAINED
1	HARD-COOKED EGG, CHOPPED

SAVORY BROCCOLI SALAD

Trim broccoli and cut stalks lengthwise into bite-size pieces. Steam florets and stalks until crisp-tender, about 3-4 minutes. Drain. Rinse with cold water. Drain and place in 1 layer in a shallow pan.

Mix oil, vinegar, salt, pepper, basil, mustard and garlic and pour over broccoli. Marinate at room temperature for 5 hours, or overnight, refrigerated.

Drain broccoli from marinade and place on a serving platter. Reserve 1 teaspoon each pimento and capers as garnish. Mix together mayonnaise, sour cream, pimentos and capers.

Spoon mayonnaise mixture over broccoli. Top with chopped egg, capers and pimento. *Yield: 4 servings.*

1	TABLESPOON VEGETABLE OIL
1½	CUPS BULGUR (CRACKED WHEAT)
3½	CUPS BOILING WATER
2	TEASPOONS SALT
½	CUP KASHA (TOASTED BUCKWHEAT GROATS)
1	EGG, LIGHTLY BEATEN
⅓	POUND HAM, JULIENNED
9	SCALLIONS, SLICED
⅔	CUP EXTRA VIRGIN OLIVE OIL
⅓	CUP SHERRY VINEGAR OR RED WINE VINEGAR
	SALT AND FRESHLY GROUND PEPPER TO TASTE

BULGUR AND KASHA SALAD

In a saucepan add oil and bulgur. Toast bulgur until hot and beginning to crackle. Remove pan from heat and add 3 cups boiling water and 1 teaspoon salt. Cover and simmer 20-25 minutes or until liquid is absorbed. Cool.

In a bowl mix kasha with half the beaten egg. In a skillet, over high heat, toss kasha until egg coating is dry and all grains separate. Add remaining boiling water and salt. Cover. Reduce heat to low, cooking until liquid is absorbed, about 15 minutes. Add bulgur. Cool.

Add remaining ingredients and toss. Serve at room temperature. *Yield: 8 servings.*

1	LARGE CELERY ROOT, PEELED, JULIENNED, BLANCHED AND DRAINED
6	LARGE CELERY STALKS, JULIENNED
½	POUND GRUYÈRE CHEESE, JULIENNED
1	CUP MAYONNAISE
1	TABLESPOON COARSE DIJON MUSTARD
	JUICE OF 1 LEMON
	SALT AND FRESHLY GROUND PEPPER
½	CUP FINELY MINCED, FRESH MIXED HERBS (DILL, CHIVES, TARRAGON OR PARSLEY)
6	LARGE LEAVES FROM 1 HEAD OF BIBB LETTUCE, CLEANED AND STEMMED

CELERIAC AND GRUYÈRE SALAD

In a large bowl toss together celery root, celery and cheese.

In another bowl combine mayonnaise, mustard, lemon juice, salt and pepper. Add to salad. Mix well. Stir in herbs and chill until ready to serve.

Place one lettuce leaf on each plate and top with salad. Serve slightly chilled. *Yield: 6 servings.*

½   BUNCH RED LEAF LETTUCE
½   BUNCH WATERCRESS
1   HEAD BIBB LETTUCE
4   OUNCES WALNUT MEATS,
     COARSELY CHOPPED
½   CUP JICAMA, CUBED
8   OUNCES MANDARIN
     ORANGES, DRAINED
2   OUNCES EDIBLE FLOWERS:
     VIOLETS, NASTURTIUM,
     PANSIES AND/OR ROSE PETALS
RASPBERRY VINAIGRETTE
1   GARLIC CLOVE
⅓   CUP RASPBERRY VINEGAR
1   EGG YOLK
2   TEASPOONS DIJON MUSTARD
    SALT AND FRESHLY GROUND
     PEPPER TO TASTE
1   CUP VEGETABLE OIL

EDIBLE FLOWER SALAD

Preheat oven to 375° F. Wash and pat dry all greens.

Toast walnut meats in oven for 5-10 minutes, until lightly browned.

For dressing, in a food processor or blender process the garlic. Add remaining ingredients, except oil, and process to blend. With the machine running, add oil in a slow, steady stream and process until thickened.

Mix all ingredients except flowers and toss lightly with dressing.

Top with edible flower assortment and serve immediately.

Yield: 4 to 6 servings.

2   TABLESPOONS FRESHLY
     SQUEEZED LEMON JUICE
½   CUP EXTRA VIRGIN OLIVE OIL
    LARGE PINCH OF KOSHER
     SALT DISSOLVED IN 2
     TABLESPOONS LEMON JUICE
    FRESHLY GROUND PEPPER
1   HEAD RADICCHIO,
     CLEANED, STEMMED AND
     COARSELY CHOPPED
2   BELGIAN ENDIVES, CLEANED
     AND CUT INTO THIRDS ON
     THE DIAGONAL
1   FENNEL BULB, CORED AND CUT
     INTO LENGTHWISE STRIPS
    LEAVES FROM 1 SMALL BUNCH
     ITALIAN PARSLEY
¼   POUND FRESHLY GRATED
     PARMESAN CHEESE

ENDIVE SALAD WITH PARMESAN

In a small bowl, whisk together 2 tablespoons lemon juice and olive oil, add dissolved salt and pepper.

Toss with remaining ingredients and serve immediately.

Yield: 4 servings.

....

SAUTERNES SUMMER FRUIT SALAD

1	QUART FRESH STRAWBERRIES, HULLED
1	PINT FRESH RASPBERRIES
1	PINT FRESH BLUEBERRIES
½	POUND BING CHERRIES, PITTED
4	PEACHES, PITTED, THINLY SLICED
3	TABLESPOONS SUGAR
5	TABLESPOONS SAUTERNES
3	TABLESPOONS FRESHLY SQUEEZED ORANGE JUICE
	MINT AS GARNISH

In a bowl gently toss all ingredients except mint.

Serve in chilled goblets garnished with a sprig of fresh mint. *Yield: 8 to 10 servings.*

....

GREEK PEASANT SALAD

1	HEAD ROMAINE LETTUCE
1	LARGE TOMATO, SLICED
1	CUCUMBER, SEEDED, THINLY SLICED
1	GREEN PEPPER, CORED, SEEDED, SLICED INTO STRIPS
1	MEDIUM RED ONION, THINLY SLICED
½	POUND GREEK OLIVES, PITTED AND HALVED
½	POUND FETA CHEESE, CRUMBLED

VINAIGRETTE DRESSING

½	CUP EXTRA VIRGIN OLIVE OIL
2	TABLESPOONS RED WINE VINEGAR
1	LARGE CLOVE GARLIC, CRUSHED
1	TEASPOON FRESH OREGANO, CHOPPED
1	TEASPOON FRESH THYME LEAVES
	SALT AND FRESHLY GROUND PEPPER

Place lettuce leaves on a large serving platter. Top with vegetables, olives and cheese.

In small bowl whisk together dressing ingredients and drizzle over salad. *Yield: 4 to 6 servings.*

1½	PINTS CHERRY TOMATOES, HALVED
¼	CUP PACKED, FRESH BASIL LEAVES
6	OUNCES SMOKED MOZZARELLA, CUT INTO ½″ SQUARES
2	TABLESPOONS WHITE WINE VINEGAR
	SALT AND FRESHLY GROUND PEPPER TO TASTE
⅓	CUP EXTRA VIRGIN OLIVE OIL

BASIL TOMATO SALAD WITH SMOKED MOZZARELLA

In a bowl combine the tomato, basil and cheese.

In another bowl whisk together the vinegar, salt and pepper. Add the oil in a steady stream, whisking, until thoroughly combined.

Toss with salad ingredients. Cover and chill. Bring to room temperature before serving. *Yield: 6 servings.*

1	POUND SMALL RED POTATOES
¼	CUP DRY WHITE WINE
1	TABLESPOON WHITE WINE VINEGAR
3	TABLESPOONS LIGHT OLIVE OIL
	SALT AND FRESHLY GROUND PEPPER
1½	TABLESPOONS MINCED FRESH TARRAGON
1½	TABLESPOONS MINCED FRESH CHERVIL
1½	TABLESPOONS MINCED FRESH CHIVES

FRENCH POTATO SALAD

Cook the potatoes in lightly salted, boiling water until tender, about 15-20 minutes. Drain. Cut potatoes into ½″ slices. Toss gently with wine and allow to steep a few minutes.

Whisk together vinegar, olive oil, salt and pepper and add to potatoes. Toss gently. Correct seasonings.

Just before serving, toss gently with the herbs. Serve warm or at room temperature. *Yield: 4 servings.*

2	POUNDS SMALL NEW POTATOES, SLICED ⅓″ THICK
¾	CUP SOUR CREAM
¼	CUP MAYONNAISE
⅓	POUND THINLY SLICED, SMOKED SALMON, CUT INTO 2″ STRIPS
1	TABLESPOON PREPARED HORSERADISH
1	TABLESPOON CAPERS
½	CUP CHOPPED, FRESH DILL

POTATO SALAD WITH SMOKED SALMON

In a saucepan boil potatoes in lightly salted water for 10 minutes or until tender. Drain and plunge potatoes into cold water to stop cooking. Drain; pat dry.

In a serving bowl combine the remaining ingredients. Add potatoes and toss gently. *Yield: 4 to 6 servings.*

1	TABLESPOON SESAME SEEDS
½	POUND FRESH SNOW PEAS
2	CUPS CHERRY TOMATOES, HALVED
¼	POUND MUSHROOMS, HALVED
4	OUNCES SLICED WATER CHESTNUTS, DRAINED
	DRESSING
2	TABLESPOONS WHITE WINE VINEGAR
2	TABLESPOONS SUGAR
1½	TEASPOONS SOY SAUCE
1	TEASPOON FRESH GINGER ROOT, PEELED AND GRATED
⅓	CUP VEGETABLE OIL

SNOW PEA SALAD WITH GINGER DRESSING

In a small skillet, toast sesame seeds over medium heat until light brown, 1-2 minutes. Shake skillet frequently to keep seeds from burning.

For dressing, combine vinegar, sugar, soy sauce and ginger in blender or food processor. With motor running, add oil in slow, steady stream and blend until mixture is thick and smooth.

Trim stem end of snow peas, pulling along pod to remove string. Bring a large pot of water to a boil, add snow peas and boil uncovered until crisp-tender, about 2 minutes. Drain, immerse in ice water and drain again.

In a salad bowl combine snow peas, tomatoes, mushrooms and water chestnuts. Sprinkle with toasted sesame seeds and toss with dressing. Cover bowl and refrigerate until ready to serve, up to 2 hours. *Yield: 4 servings.*

1	POUND FRESH SPINACH, STEMS TRIMMED
2	CUPS SLICED FRESH STRAWBERRIES
4	OUNCES CHEDDAR CHEESE, SHREDDED
	DRESSING
⅓	CUP VEGETABLE OIL
3	TABLESPOONS RED WINE VINEGAR
2	TEASPOONS FRESHLY SQUEEZED LEMON JUICE
1	TEASPOON FRESHLY GRATED GINGER ROOT

STRAWBERRY SPINACH SALAD

For dressing in a large salad bowl blend oil, vinegar, lemon juice and ginger.

Add spinach, strawberries and cheese. Toss and serve immediately. *Yield: 8 to 10 servings.*

1	CUP CAULIFLOWER FLORETS
1	CUP BROCCOLI FLORETS
3	OUNCES GREEN BEANS, TRIMMED
⅓	SWEET RED PEPPER, CUT INTO STRIPS
⅓	YELLOW PEPPER, CUT INTO STRIPS
12	OUNCES HEARTS OF PALM, DRAINED, CUT INTO ½″ DIAGONAL SLICES
5	OUNCES FRESH SPINACH, WASHED, STEMS REMOVED, PATTED DRY
	DRESSING
⅓	CUP EXTRA VIRGIN OLIVE OIL
3	TABLESPOONS RED WINE VINEGAR
¾	TABLESPOON DIJON MUSTARD
¾	TEASPOON SUGAR
¼	TEASPOON SALT
¼	TEASPOON FRESHLY GROUND PEPPER
¼	TEASPOON OREGANO
¼	TEASPOON MINCED GARLIC

MARINATED VEGETABLE SALAD WITH DIJON DRESSING

In a large pan bring 1½ quarts water to a boil. Drop cauliflower and broccoli into boiling water. Cook 4 minutes. Remove florets with slotted spoon. Drain and rinse under cold water. Drain again.

Return water to a boil and add green beans. Cook 2 minutes. Remove, drain, rinse with cold water. Drain again.

Combine all vegetables except spinach. Set aside.

Put dressing ingredients into container with tight fitting lid and shake well. Pour dressing over vegetables and toss to mix. Refrigerate 2-3 hours.

Prepare bed of spinach on platter. Spoon vegetables over.
Yield: 4 servings.

6	BUNCHES WATERCRESS, CLEANED AND STEMMED
16	WATER CHESTNUTS, FINELY CHOPPED
1½	TEASPOONS LIGHT SOY SAUCE
1½	TABLESPOONS SESAME OIL
½	TEASPOON SUGAR
½	TEASPOON SALT

WATERCRESS AND WATER CHESTNUT SALAD

In a large saucepan bring 4 cups water to a boil. Drop watercress into the boiling water to blanch. Stir once or twice and then drain the watercress in a colander. Run under cold water to stop cooking process. Squeeze excess liquid from watercress with paper towel. Chop finely and place in a bowl with water chestnuts.

In a separate bowl combine remaining ingredients. Add to the salad mixture. Toss and serve. *Yield: 6 servings.*

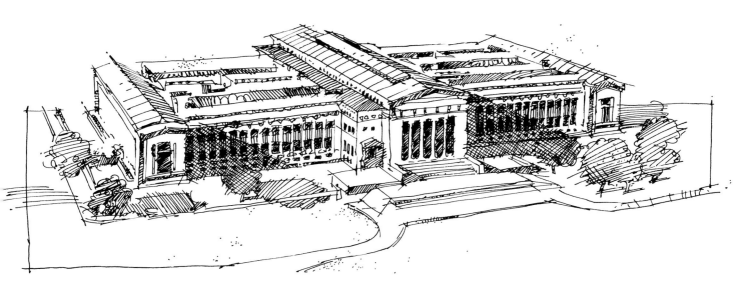

THE FIELD MUSEUM OF NATURAL HISTORY, designed by Daniel H. Burnham, was constructed from 1911 to 1919. The largest Georgian marble structure in the world, it was built and is partially maintained by funds from Marshall Field I. The museum is a showcase for prehistoric and recent cultures, featuring exhibits from the fields of anthropology, botany, geology and zoology.

¾ CUP EXTRA VIRGIN OLIVE OIL
¼ CUP RASPBERRY VINEGAR
1 TABLESPOON DIJON MUSTARD
  FRESHLY SQUEEZED
   LEMON JUICE
1 LARGE AVOCADO, PEELED,
  PITTED AND SLICED
4 CUPS RARE SIRLOIN STRIPS
2 CUPS SLICED RAW MUSHROOMS
1 CUP SLICED RED PEPPER
1 CUP SLICED YELLOW PEPPER
1 CUP SNOW PEAS, BLANCHED
4 CUPS ESCAROLE, TORN INTO
  SMALL PIECES
2 HARD-COOKED EGGS, DICED

BEEF, PEPPER AND AVOCADO SALAD

In a small bowl mix together oil, vinegar and mustard. Let dressing stand at room temperature for 1 hour.

Squeeze lemon juice over avocado and set aside.

Combine all remaining ingredients. Toss gently with dressing. Serve garnished with avocado. *Yield: 6 servings.*

2 POUNDS BEEF TENDERLOIN
⅓ CUP TERIYAKI SAUCE
1 POUND FRESH SNOW PEA PODS
¾ POUND FRESH SPINACH LEAVES,
  WASHED, STEMMED AND
  PATTED DRY
1 PINT CHERRY TOMATOES
 CHINESE NOODLES
 DRESSING
½ CUP FRESHLY SQUEEZED
  LEMON JUICE
6 TABLESPOONS LIGHT
  SOY SAUCE
¼ CUP EXTRA VIRGIN OLIVE OIL
2 TABLESPOONS SESAME OIL
4 THIN SLICES FRESH GINGER
  ROOT, PEELED AND MINCED
1½ TEASPOONS SUGAR
⅓ TEASPOON WHITE PEPPER

COLD CHINESE BEEF SALAD

Brush steak with teriyaki sauce. Cover and refrigerate for 2½ hours.

Combine dressing ingredients in container with tightly fitting lid. Shake well to mix. *Preheat broiler.*

Broil steak until medium-rare or to desired doneness, about 6-8 minutes. Cool and slice across the grain into thin strips.

Blanch pea pods in boiling water for 30 seconds. Drain. Rinse under cold water. Drain again.

Combine pea pods with beef. Add dressing and toss.

Arrange spinach leaves on serving platter. Top with salad mixture. Garnish with cherry tomatoes and sprinkle with Chinese noodles. *Yield: 6 servings.*

2	WHOLE CHICKEN BREASTS, BONED AND SKINNED
3	CUPS CHICKEN BROTH
1	CUP DRY WHITE WINE
½	CUP SLICED WATER CHESTNUTS
¾	CUP FRESH PEA PODS, BLANCHED
1	GRANNY SMITH APPLE, CORED AND DICED
1	RIPE PEAR, CORED AND DICED
1	PINCH GRATED LEMON RIND
1	TABLESPOON FRESHLY SQUEEZED LEMON JUICE
1	CUP MAYONNAISE
1	CUP CHINESE NOODLES

ORIENTAL CHICKEN SALAD

Poach chicken breasts in broth and wine. Drain and let cool 30 minutes. Cut into bite-size pieces.

In a bowl combine water chestnuts, pea pods, apple and pear with chicken.

Mix lemon rind and juice with mayonnaise. Add to chicken mixture and stir gently to coat.

Serve topped with Chinese noodles. *Yield: 4 servings.*

2	TABLESPOONS VEGETABLE OIL
¾	POUND CHICKEN BREASTS, CUT INTO ¾″ CUBES
2	SCALLIONS, CUT DIAGONALLY INTO ½″ LENGTHS
2	TABLESPOONS DRY VERMOUTH
	SALT AND FRESHLY GROUND PEPPER
1	TEASPOON CORNSTARCH
¼	CUP CHICKEN BROTH
2	TABLESPOONS FRESHLY SQUEEZED LEMON JUICE
1	AVOCADO, PEELED, PITTED AND CUBED
4	SLICES BACON, COOKED AND CRUMBLED
	BIBB LETTUCE

LEMON CHICKEN SALAD WITH AVOCADO AND BACON

Heat oil in wok or skillet over medium-high heat. Stir-fry chicken and scallions until chicken loses its pink color, about 1 minute. Add vermouth and stir-fry 1 minute more. Season with salt and pepper to taste.

Mix cornstarch with broth. Add broth mixture and lemon juice to ingredients in wok. Stir-fry until broth thickens, about 2 minutes. Remove from heat. Toss with avocado and crumbled bacon. Serve in lettuce cups. *Yield: 4 servings.*

2   LARGE DUCKS
       (4-5 POUNDS EACH)
1   CUP EXTRA VIRGIN OLIVE OIL
2   TABLESPOONS RED
       WINE VINEGAR
2   TABLESPOONS FRESHLY
       SQUEEZED LEMON JUICE
4   TEASPOONS DIJON MUSTARD
4   TEASPOONS SOY SAUCE
2   TABLESPOONS SESAME SEEDS
1   HEAD ROMAINE LETTUCE,
       WASHED, SEPARATED
       AND TORN INTO
       BITE-SIZE PIECES

DUCK SALAD WITH SESAME DRESSING

Preheat oven to 375° F. Roast duck on rack in pan for 45 minutes or until juices run clear when pierced in the thickest part. Let cool. Discard skin and cut meat into thin strips.

In a bowl mix together olive oil, vinegar, lemon juice, mustard, soy sauce, sesame seeds and any defatted juices from the ducks.

Toss duck with dressing and serve on a bed of romaine.
Yield: 6 servings.

24   JULIENNED STRIPS OF RARE,
       COLD LAMB
3   BUNCHES BELGIAN ENDIVE,
       SEPARATED INTO LEAVES
1   CUP SLICED RAW FENNEL
2   TABLESPOONS FENNEL FRONDS
1   CUP SWEET RED PEPPER, CUT
       IN STRIPS
1   CUP YELLOW PEPPER, CUT
       IN STRIPS
6   OUNCES GOAT CHEESE,
       THINLY SLICED
       APRICOT DRESSING
1   TABLESPOON APRICOT JAM
¾   CUP PEANUT OIL
¼   CUP RASPBERRY VINEGAR
       PINCH OF FRESH DILL

LAMB AND FENNEL SALAD

Combine all salad ingredients. Chill.

Combine all dressing ingredients in a container with a tightly fitting lid. Shake well to mix. Let stand at room temperature for 1 hour before serving.

Toss salad with dressing. *Yield: 6 servings.*

2	CLOVES GARLIC, MINCED
1	TABLESPOON EXTRA VIRGIN OLIVE OIL
1	POUND UNCOOKED SPAGHETTI
1½	POUNDS SHREDDED MOZZARELLA CHEESE
6	TOMATOES, PEELED AND CHOPPED
3	BUNCHES WATERCRESS, CHOPPED
1½	POUNDS FRESH SNOW PEAS, BLANCHED
16	OUNCES FRESH PEAS, COOKED UNTIL TENDER
1	POUND FRESH SHRIMP, SHELLED, DEVEINED AND COOKED
	PARMESAN CHEESE, FRESHLY GRATED

PASTA SALAD WITH MOZZARELLA AND SHRIMP

In a large pot, sauté garlic in oil. Remove garlic and set aside.

In same large pot cook spaghetti in boiling water for 7 minutes until al dente. Drain and return spaghetti to the pot.

Add mozzarella, stirring until it melts.

Add garlic and remaining ingredients, except for the Parmesan cheese. Toss lightly. Sprinkle with Parmesan cheese and serve at room temperature. *Yield: 12 servings.*

⅓	POUND ARUGULA, WASHED
1	RED PEPPER, CUT INTO STRIPS
1	YELLOW PEPPER, CUT INTO STRIPS
4	TABLESPOONS BUTTER
1	POUND FRESH BAY SCALLOPS
1	SMALL CLOVE GARLIC, MINCED
	ITALIAN PARSLEY AS GARNISH
	SHERRY VINAIGRETTE DRESSING
1	TABLESPOON SHERRY WINE VINEGAR
1	TEASPOON FRESHLY SQUEEZED LEMON JUICE
1	TABLESPOON WALNUT OIL
⅓	CUP EXTRA VIRGIN OLIVE OIL
	SALT AND FRESHLY GROUND PEPPER

WARM SALAD OF SCALLOPS, PEPPERS AND ARUGULA

For the dressing, in a small bowl whisk together vinegar and lemon juice. Slowly add the oils in a steady stream, whisking until combined. Season with salt and pepper to taste.

Toss the arugula and peppers with enough vinaigrette to coat them lightly. Divide them among salad plates.

Melt the butter in a sauté pan. Add the scallops and garlic. Sauté, stirring constantly, for 1 minute or until the scallops are slightly golden. Remove the scallops from the pan with a slotted spoon and place on top of mixture on salad plates.

Add remaining vinaigrette to sauté pan and warm through. Spoon over each salad. Garnish with Italian parsley. *Yield: 6 servings.*

2 CUPS PESTO TORTELLINI PASTA
1 POUND MEDIUM SHRIMP
½ POUND CHINESE PEA PODS
¼ CUP FRESHLY GRATED
    PARMESAN CHEESE
4 SCALLIONS, CHOPPED
  SALT AND FRESHLY
    GROUND PEPPER
½ CUP MAYONNAISE
  ROMAINE LETTUCE
  FRESH BASIL

SHRIMP AND TORTELLINI SALAD WITH BASIL

Cook pasta until al dente, about 7 minutes. Drain and rinse. Set aside.

Boil shrimp in shells 2 minutes and drain. Let cool and peel.

Blanch pea pods about 2 minutes in boiling water. Drain and rinse in cold water to delay further cooking. Drain again.

Combine pasta, shrimp, pea pods, cheese, scallions, salt, pepper and mayonnaise. Chill.

Serve on romaine lettuce. Sprinkle with fresh basil.

Yield: 4 to 6 servings.

8 OUNCES LONG-GRAIN
    BROWN RICE
4 OUNCES WILD RICE
1 RED BELL PEPPER, DICED
1 GREEN BELL PEPPER, DICED
1 POUND SHRIMP, COOKED,
    COOLED AND PEELED
½ CUP DICED RED ONION
½ CUP BLACK OLIVES, PITTED
    AND SLICED
½ CUP CELERY, DICED
2 TABLESPOONS CHOPPED
    FRESH PARSLEY
4 RIPE AVOCADOS AS GARNISH
  FRESH LEMON JUICE
3 RIPE TOMATOES, SLICED,
    AS GARNISH
  DRESSING
½ CUP VEGETABLE OIL
¼ CUP WHITE WINE VINEGAR
2 TEASPOONS DIJON MUSTARD
1 TEASPOON SUGAR
½ TEASPOON SALT
½ TEASPOON FRESHLY
    GROUND PEPPER

SHRIMP AND VEGETABLE SALAD

Cook each rice separately according to package directions. Place in a large bowl and set aside.

Combine peppers, shrimp, onion, olives, celery and parsley. Set aside.

Combine dressing ingredients in a container with a tightly fitting lid and shake well to blend. Pour over rice. Add vegetables to rice mixture. Toss. Cover and refrigerate several hours or overnight.

Peel and slice avocados. Sprinkle with fresh lemon juice.

Serve salad garnished with avocados and tomatoes.

Yield: 6 to 8 servings.

2	POUNDS BONELESS SIRLOIN, 2″ THICK
	SALT AND FRESHLY GROUND PEPPER
¾	POUND NEW POTATOES, COOKED AND QUARTERED
12	OUNCES HEARTS OF PALM, SLICED 1″ THICK
1	SMALL RED ONION, PEELED AND SLICED
1	SMALL RED BELL PEPPER, SLICED IN SLIVERS
1	SMALL GREEN BELL PEPPER, SLICED IN SLIVERS
4	TABLESPOONS CHOPPED FRESH CHIVES
3	TABLESPOONS CHOPPED FRESH PARSLEY
	ROMAINE LETTUCE LEAVES
	SNOW PEAS, SLICED MUSHROOMS AND CHERRY TOMATOES AS GARNISH
	MUSTARD VINAIGRETTE DRESSING
1	EGG, BEATEN
⅓	CUP EXTRA VIRGIN OLIVE OIL
2	TEASPOONS DIJON MUSTARD
1½	TEASPOONS FRESHLY SQUEEZED LEMON JUICE
3	TABLESPOONS TARRAGON VINEGAR
1	TEASPOON WORCESTERSHIRE SAUCE
1	TEASPOON SALT
	FRESHLY GROUND PEPPER TO TASTE

STEAK SALAD WITH MUSTARD VINAIGRETTE

Preheat broiler. Season steak with salt and pepper and broil to desired doneness. Cool and slice thinly into bite-size pieces.

Combine with salad ingredients except romaine and garnishes. Toss gently.

Combine dressing ingredients in a container with a tightly fitting lid and shake well to blend.

Pour vinaigrette dressing over salad and refrigerate for 3-4 hours.

Serve over romaine lettuce leaves with snow peas, mushrooms and cherry tomatoes. *Yield: 8 to 10 servings.*

FORT DEARBORN, a military outpost established by President Thomas Jefferson, was once located here. Markers imbedded in the sidewalk pavement outline the perimeters of the fort. The Fort Dearborn Massacre of 1812 is commemorated by plaques and sculptures on the bridge towers. The original street level for this area of Chicago was actually at the river's surface. Time and high-rise construction have created a street level that is artificially high. Chicago has adapted to both levels by creating double-decked roads along stretches of Wacker Drive and Michigan Avenue.

10 OUNCES FRESH ANGEL HAIR
    PASTA
1½ CUPS RICOTTA CHEESE
3 EGGS
1½ TEASPOONS SALT
¼ TEASPOON FRESHLY GROUND
    BLACK PEPPER
8-10 DROPS HOT RED
    PEPPER SAUCE
1½ CUPS MILK
4 TEASPOONS UNSALTED BUTTER

ANGEL HAIR PASTA IN RICOTTA CUSTARD

Preheat oven to 350° F. Cook pasta in a pot of boiling, lightly salted water for 2½ minutes. Drain and rinse with cold water. Place pasta in an oiled 6-cup casserole dish.

In a medium bowl beat cheese and eggs together. Stir in salt, pepper and red pepper sauce. Add milk and mix thoroughly. Add to pasta in casserole and dot with butter.

Place casserole on cookie sheet and bake 40-45 minutes until top becomes puffy and golden in color and a knife inserted in center comes out clean. Serve immediately. *Yield: 6 to 8 servings.*

SAUCE
2 TABLESPOONS MINCED
    SHALLOTS
¼ CUP DRY VERMOUTH
2 TABLESPOONS TAMARI
¼ CUP WHIPPING CREAM
¾ CUP UNSALTED BUTTER
FILLING
½ CUP GROUND CHICKEN
⅓ CUP GOAT CHEESE, CRUMBLED
1 TEASPOON FRESH GINGER
    ROOT, FINELY MINCED
2 TABLESPOONS MINCED
    GREEN ONIONS
    WHITE PEPPER
    PINCH OF SALT
RAVIOLI
1 EGG, BEATEN
1 TEASPOON WATER
24 WONTON WRAPPERS
POACHING
2½ CUPS CHICKEN STOCK
GARNISH
    CHERVIL OR PARSLEY SPRIGS

CHICKEN AND GOAT CHEESE WONTON RAVIOLI

To make the sauce, in a saucepan, over medium heat, combine shallots, vermouth and tamari. Cook until reduced to about 2 tablespoons. Add cream and cook until reduced to 2 tablespoons. Over low heat, whisk in butter a tablespoon at a time, until melted. Set aside.

In a bowl mix the filling ingredients and set aside.

To make ravioli, beat the egg with the water and a pinch of salt. Set aside. Place a rounded teaspoon of filling in each wonton wrapper. Paint the edges with the egg wash. Cover with another wrapper and press around the edges to remove air and seal well. Cut off excess dough with a crimping design.

In a large frying pan heat the chicken stock to a simmer. Poach the wonton ravioli in the simmering stock 4 minutes or until centers are translucent.

Ladle sauce on warmed plates. With a slotted spoon remove ravioli from poaching liquid and place in the sauce. Garnish with chervil or parsley. *Yield: 4 servings.*

6	TABLESPOONS BUTTER
¼	POUND FONTINA CHEESE, CUT INTO ¼" CUBES
¼	POUND GORGONZOLA CHEESE, CUT INTO ¼" CUBES
¼	POUND MOZZARELLA CHEESE, CUT INTO ¼" CUBES
1½	POUNDS MEDIUM OR FINE GREEN AND WHITE PASTA
1	CUP FRESHLY GRATED PARMESAN CHEESE
1	CUP WHIPPING CREAM
	SALT AND FRESHLY GROUND PEPPER

GREEN AND WHITE PASTA WITH FOUR CHEESES

In a large saucepan heat the butter. Add fontina, Gorgonzola and mozzarella cheeses. Cook over low heat, stirring constantly, until cheeses have melted. Keep warm over lowest possible heat.

Cook the pasta in rapidly boiling, salted water, stirring frequently, for 5-10 minutes or until al dente.

While pasta is cooking, add the Parmesan to the cheese sauce, stirring until it is melted. Stir in the cream and heat thoroughly but do not boil. Correct the seasoning.

Drain pasta thoroughly and toss with the cheese sauce. Serve immediately. *Yield: 4 to 6 servings.*

½	POUND FRESH LINGUINE
3	TABLESPOONS BUTTER
½	CUP CHOPPED LEEKS, WHITE PART ONLY
½	CUP THINLY SLICED RED BELL PEPPER
8	OUNCES BAY SCALLOPS
4	OUNCES GOAT CHEESE
1½	TABLESPOONS WHIPPING CREAM
	SALT, FRESHLY GROUND PEPPER AND CAYENNE PEPPER TO TASTE
	PARSLEY, CHOPPED

LINGUINE WITH GOAT CHEESE, RED PEPPERS AND SCALLOPS

Cook pasta in boiling water until al dente. Drain.

In a large saucepan, over medium-high heat, melt 2 tablespoons of the butter. Add leeks and red peppers. Sauté until tender, about 3 minutes. Stir in scallops and remaining 1 tablespoon butter. Sauté over medium heat until scallops are opaque, about 1 minute. Stir in cheese and cream until blended and heated through. Season to taste with salt, pepper and cayenne.

Toss scallop mixture with hot pasta. Sprinkle with parsley and serve immediately. *Yield: 2 servings.*

1   MEDIUM ONION, CHOPPED
2   SLICES UNCOOKED
      BACON, DICED
3   TABLESPOONS EXTRA VIRGIN
      OLIVE OIL
1   POUND RIPE TOMATOES,
      PEELED AND CHOPPED
1   BAY LEAF
    SALT AND FRESHLY GROUND
      PEPPER TO TASTE
⅓   CUP COGNAC
⅓   CUP WHIPPING CREAM
1   POUND RIGATONI PASTA
1   CUP GRATED CHEDDAR CHEESE

PASTA WITH COGNAC

In a saucepan combine onion and bacon with oil and cook until softened, about 4 minutes. Add the tomatoes, bay leaf, salt and pepper and simmer for 30 minutes, stirring occasionally.

Transfer mixture to a food processor and purée. Return to saucepan and stir in cognac. Add cream and warm gently.

Cook pasta in boiling, salted water until al dente, about 8 minutes. Drain and set aside.

Add tomato sauce and ½ of the grated cheese to the pasta. Toss until well blended. Add salt and pepper to taste.

Serve on a platter with remaining cheese sprinkled over top.
Yield: 6 to 8 servings.

5   CUPS FINELY
      CHOPPED TOMATOES
3   CLOVES GARLIC, FINELY MINCED
¼   CUP MINCED FRESH BASIL
2   TEASPOONS SALT
2   TABLESPOONS MINCED
      FRESH OREGANO
7   TABLESPOONS EXTRA VIRGIN
      OLIVE OIL
¼   POUND FONTINA CHEESE, CUT
      INTO 1″ CUBES
    JUICE OF ONE LEMON
    SALT AND FRESHLY
      GROUND PEPPER
½   POUND PENNE, COOKED
      AL DENTE
½   POUND FUSILI, COOKED
      AL DENTE
½   POUND ROTINI, COOKED
      AL DENTE
    FRESH BASIL LEAVES AS GARNISH

THREE PASTAS WITH FRESH TOMATO SAUCE

In a large bowl combine tomatoes and their juices, garlic, basil, salt, oregano and olive oil. Mix well. Add cheese. Cover and marinate at room temperature 1 hour. Just before serving add lemon juice, salt and pepper.

Serve over piping hot pasta garnished with basil.
Yield: 8 servings.

4	TABLESPOONS PEANUT OIL
1½	POUNDS SEAFOOD (SHRIMP, SCALLOPS, LOBSTER OR MUSSELS)
4	GREEN ONIONS, FINELY CHOPPED
2	CLOVES GARLIC, MINCED
½	CUP SUN-DRIED TOMATOES IN OIL, THINLY SLICED
⅔	CUP DRY WHITE WINE
1¼	CUPS WHIPPING CREAM
2	TABLESPOONS CHOPPED FRESH BASIL
½	POUND FRESH SNOW PEAS, STEAMED UNTIL CRISP-TENDER
½	POUND LINGUINE, COOKED AL DENTE
2	TABLESPOONS MINCED FRESH PARSLEY

PASTA WITH SEAFOOD AND SUN-DRIED TOMATOES

In a wok, over medium-high heat, add oil and stir-fry seafood until just cooked, 2-3 minutes. Remove seafood with slotted spoon and set aside.

Add green onions, garlic and tomatoes and stir-fry until soft, about 2-3 minutes. Add wine and continue cooking another 3 minutes. Add cream, basil and snow peas, cooking until mixture thickens, about 3 minutes.

Serve pasta topped with seafood, sauce and parsley.
Yield: 4 servings.

¼	CUP OYSTER SAUCE
2	TABLESPOONS HONEY
2	TEASPOONS CHILI OIL
1	EGG YOLK
1	TABLESPOON HOISIN SAUCE
2	TEASPOONS FISH SAUCE
2	WHOLE BONELESS, SKINNED CHICKEN BREASTS, CUT INTO BITE-SIZE CUBES
6	SMALL CARROTS, PEELED AND JULIENNED
8	OUNCES FETTUCINE
6	LARGE GREEN ONIONS, JULIENNED
1¼	CUPS FRESH CILANTRO LEAVES, MINCED
¾	CUP UNSALTED DRY-ROASTED PEANUTS, CHOPPED
3	TABLESPOONS RICE VINEGAR

SPICY NOODLES WITH PEANUTS AND CHICKEN

In a large saucepan, over medium heat, combine oyster sauce, honey, chili oil, egg yolk, hoisin sauce and fish sauce. When mixture is hot add chicken and stir often until meat is firm, about 4 minutes. Set aside.

Bring 6 quarts of salted water to a boil. Add carrots and cook about 3 minutes. Remove carrots with a slotted spoon and rinse under cool water. Add to chicken mixture.

Return liquid to a boil, add fettucine and cook to al dente. Drain and return pasta to pot.

Combine chicken mixture, green onions, cilantro, peanuts and rice vinegar. Add to pasta. Toss and adjust seasonings. Serve immediately. *Yield: 6 servings.*

1 TABLESPOON BUTTER
⅓ CUP EXTRA VIRGIN OLIVE OIL
3 CLOVES GARLIC, CUT IN HALF
2 POUNDS RIPE PLUM TOMATOES, PEELED AND CHOPPED
7 OUNCES SMALL MUSHROOMS, QUARTERED
1 LARGE SPRIG FRESH ROSEMARY, MINCED
6 FRESH BASIL LEAVES, CHOPPED
1 CUP SHELLED PEAS
PINCH OF CAYENNE PEPPER
SALT AND FRESHLY GROUND PEPPER TO TASTE
1 POUND UNCOOKED RIGATONI
⅓ CUP WHIPPING CREAM
¾ CUP FRESHLY GRATED PARMESAN CHEESE

RIGATONI ALLA MEDICI

In a saucepan heat the butter and olive oil with the garlic. When the garlic is lightly browned, remove it with a slotted spoon.

Add the tomatoes and simmer for 10 minutes. Add mushrooms and simmer 5 minutes. Add rosemary, basil, peas, cayenne pepper, salt and black pepper and simmer 5 minutes.

In a large pot of boiling water add salt and then rigatoni. Cook to al dente, about 8 minutes. Drain and transfer to a serving platter.

Add cream to sauce and cook, stirring occasionally until heated.

Pour hot sauce over pasta, add half of the Parmesan and toss. Serve with remaining Parmesan sprinkled on top. *Yield: 6 servings.*

1 TEASPOON LIGHT OLIVE OIL
¼ POUND PANCETTA, CUT INTO ½″ CUBES
1 SMALL ONION, MINCED
1 GARLIC CLOVE, MINCED
1 CUP DRY WHITE WINE
3 TABLESPOONS TOMATO PASTE
6 MEDIUM TOMATOES PEELED, SEEDED AND CHOPPED
4 OUNCES RADICCHIO, CORED AND CUT INTO ⅜″ RIBBONS
¼ CUP EXTRA VIRGIN OLIVE OIL
¼ TEASPOON SALT
FRESHLY GROUND PEPPER
½ POUND ROTINI, COOKED AL DENTE, DRAINED
¼ POUND MOZZARELLA CHEESE, GRATED

ROTINI WITH RADICCHIO, PANCETTA AND TOMATOES

Heat saucepan. When hot, add 1 teaspoon light oil and pancetta. Cook over medium heat until limp but not crisp, about 6 minutes. Add onion and garlic and continue to cook, stirring occasionally for 3-4 minutes until onion is lightly browned.

Add wine, stirring up brown pieces from bottom of pan. Cook over high heat until liquid is reduced by half, about 4 minutes. Add the tomato paste, tomatoes and ½ of the radicchio. Reduce heat to medium and cook until thickened, about 16 minutes.

Remove from heat and stir in remaining radicchio, olive oil, salt and pepper to taste.

Toss pasta with sauce. Sprinkle with cheese and serve immediately. *Yield: 6 servings.*

2	CUPS LONG-GRAIN WHITE RICE
4	FRESH STICKS MEXICAN CINNAMON
½	CUP FINELY DICED CARROTS
½	CUP FINELY DICED CELERY
½	CUP FINELY DICED WHITE ONION
½	TEASPOON SALT
4	TABLESPOONS UNSALTED BUTTER
½	CUP CURRANTS
6	CUPS WATER

MEXICAN SWEET CINNAMON RICE

Place all ingredients in a large saucepan and bring to a boil over high heat, uncovered, cooking until water level is even with the rice. Reduce heat to low, cover pan tightly and simmer until rice is tender, about 15-20 minutes.

Fluff rice with a fork, removing cinnamon sticks.

Yield: 8 servings.

4	SHALLOTS, FINELY CHOPPED
3	CLOVES GARLIC, MINCED
2½	TABLESPOONS GINGER ROOT, PEELED AND FINELY SLICED
1½	CUPS DRY SHERRY
3	CUPS WHIPPING CREAM SALT AND FRESHLY GROUND PEPPER TO TASTE
2	TABLESPOONS UNSALTED BUTTER
1	POUND SHRIMP, PEELED, DEVEINED
½	POUND SPINACH PASTA, COOKED AL DENTE, DRAINED
4	TABLESPOONS PINE NUTS
4	TABLESPOONS THICK TOMATO SAUCE

CREAMY GINGER SHRIMP WITH SPINACH PASTA

In a heavy saucepan, over medium heat, combine shallots, garlic, ginger and sherry. Simmer until mixture is reduced by two-thirds. Add cream. Simmer over medium-low heat, stirring often, until thick, about 1 hour. Transfer to food processor and purée. Strain, if desired, and season to taste with salt and freshly ground pepper.

Place a heavy saucepan, over medium heat, until hot. Add butter and melt. Add shrimp and sauté until almost tender, about 4 minutes.

Add cooked pasta and cream sauce. Cook over low heat, stirring gently.

Serve pasta encircled with shrimp. Garnish with toasted pine nuts and tomato sauce. *Yield: 4 servings.*

1 CUP WILD RICE, UNCOOKED
¼ CUP BUTTER
½ CUP SLIVERED ALMONDS
2 TABLESPOONS CHOPPED
  CHIVES OR SCALLIONS
¼ POUND FRESH
  MUSHROOMS, SLICED
3 CUPS CHICKEN BROTH

WILD RICE WITH ALMONDS AND MUSHROOMS

Preheat oven to 325° F. Wash and drain rice. Set aside.

In a large skillet melt butter. Add rice, almonds, chives and mushrooms. Cook and stir until almonds are golden brown, about 20 minutes.

Pour rice mixture into ungreased 1½ quart casserole. Heat broth to a boil and add to rice mixture. Stir and cover tightly. Bake 1½ hours or until all liquid is absorbed and rice is tender and fluffy. *Yield: 6 to 8 servings.*

2 CUPS FLOUR
½ TEASPOON SALT
3 EGGS, LIGHTLY BEATEN
3 TABLESPOONS EXTRA VIRGIN
  OLIVE OIL
6-8 OUNCES FRESH LOBSTER
3 OUNCES BONELESS, SKINLESS
  SALMON FILLETS
4 OUNCES BONELESS, SKINLESS
  RED SNAPPER FILLETS
½ TEASPOON SALT
½ TEASPOON HOT RED
  PEPPER SAUCE
1¼ CUPS WHIPPING
  CREAM, CHILLED
TOMATO CHIVE SAUCE
1 CUP CHICKEN STOCK
1 CUP UNSALTED BUTTER
  SALT AND FRESHLY
  GROUND PEPPER
¼ CUP DICED TOMATOES
2 TABLESPOONS MINCED
  FRESH CHIVES

LOBSTER RAVIOLI WITH TOMATO CHIVE SAUCE

For dough, mix flour and salt in a bowl. Make a well in the center and pour in eggs and oil. With a fork, stir until flour is moistened. Add a drop or two of water if needed. Gather into a ball. Knead dough on a lightly floured surface until it is smooth and firm. Divide into 4 pieces and wrap each piece in plastic. Let rest 45 minutes.

For the filling, place lobster, salmon, snapper, salt and red pepper sauce in a food processor. Chop finely. Transfer to a bowl. Very slowly, add enough of the cream to the fish mixture to give a thick consistency. It should be moist but not too firm. Cover and chill.

To shape pasta, pass one dough piece through a pasta machine until thin and pliable. Flour the machine and dough as required. Cut thin pasta into 1″ squares and put 1½ teaspoons of the lobster mixture in center. Top with another pasta square and pinch sides to close.

Drop raviolis into large pot of boiling water and cook until pasta is al dente, about 2 minutes. Drain.

For sauce, boil stock until reduced to about ¼ cup. Over very low heat, add butter, a tablespoon at a time, whisking until butter is melted and sauce is frothy. Do not boil. Add salt and pepper to taste. Remove sauce from heat and add tomatoes and chives. Spoon over ravioli. *Yield: 4 servings.*

24	SEA SCALLOPS, DICED
1	TEASPOON SALT
1	TEASPOON WHITE PEPPER
3	TABLESPOONS EXTRA VIRGIN OLIVE OIL
4	SPRIGS THYME
1	EGG
1	TEASPOON WATER
12	WONTON WRAPPERS, HALVED
8	OUNCES CLAM JUICE
	THYME AND PARSLEY SPRIGS AS GARNISH
	WHITE BUTTER SAUCE
1	SHALLOT, MINCED
¼	CUP DRY WHITE WINE
¼	CUP WHITE VINEGAR
2	TABLESPOONS WHIPPING CREAM
¾	CUP CHILLED UNSALTED BUTTER, DICED

SCALLOPS AND THYME RAVIOLI

In a bowl season scallops with salt and pepper. Add olive oil and thyme. Toss to mix. Marinate for 10 minutes.

To make egg wash, beat egg with water and a pinch of salt.

Make 24 ravioli by placing a teaspoon of the scallop mixture in each wonton wrapper and pressing edges to seal. Brush edges with egg wash. Cover filled ravioli with a damp towel until ready to cook.

To make the White Butter Sauce, in a small saucepan boil the shallot, wine and vinegar until liquid is reduced to about 2 tablespoons. Add the cream and reduce again to 2 tablespoons. Remove from heat and stir in the cold butter a little at a time.

In a saucepan combine clam juice and enough water to reach a depth of 2 inches. Heat to simmer. Place 1 layer of ravioli into the pan and cook about 1 minute until they rise to the surface and the dough becomes translucent. Drain and serve immediately with White Butter Sauce and a garnish of thyme and parsley sprigs.
Yield: 4 servings.

5	TABLESPOONS BUTTER
4	OUNCES FRESH CHANTERELLES OR SHIITAKE MUSHROOMS, SLICED
1	CLOVE GARLIC, FINELY MINCED
2-3	SPRIGS PARSLEY, FINELY CHOPPED
2-3	SPRIGS FRESH DILL, FINELY CHOPPED
	SALT AND FRESHLY GROUND PEPPER
4½	CUPS CHICKEN STOCK
¼	TEASPOON SALT
9	OUNCES INSTANT POLENTA
⅓	POUND MASCARPONE CHEESE

GENOA POLENTA WITH WILD MUSHROOMS

In a skillet melt 2 tablespoons of the butter. Add mushrooms and garlic and cook over low heat 1 minute. Add parsley and dill and cook 3-4 minutes longer. Season with salt and pepper. Keep warm.

In a large saucepan bring stock and salt to a boil. Gradually whisk in polenta. Lower heat and stir until thickened, about 1 minute. Just before serving, stir in remaining 3 tablespoons of butter.

Serve topped with Mascarpone and a spoonful of mushrooms.
Yield: 6 to 8 servings.

2 CUPS FLOUR
6 EGGS
1 TEASPOON SALT
½ TEASPOON CAYENNE PEPPER
⅓ CUP COLD WATER
4 TABLESPOONS BUTTER
½ CUP GRATED GRUYÈRE CHEESE
  SALT AND FRESHLY
    GROUND PEPPER

SPAETZLE WITH GRUYÈRE

In a bowl combine flour, eggs, salt, cayenne and water. Stir until batter is thoroughly mixed.

Bring a large pot of water to a boil, then place a colander on top of pot. Pour the batter into the colander and press through the holes into the simmering water. Cook for 3 minutes until the spaetzle floats to the top of the water. Remove with a slotted spoon and set aside.

When all the batter has been used, melt the butter in a sauté pan. Add spaetzle, cheese, salt and pepper. Sauté, stirring until cheese melts. *Yield: 6 servings.*

1 CUP LONG-GRAIN WHITE RICE
3 TABLESPOONS EXTRA VIRGIN
    OLIVE OIL
1 CUP DICED ONION
1 CUP DICED CELERY
1 LARGE GARLIC CLOVE, MINCED
1¾ CUPS CHICKEN STOCK
1 TABLESPOON SUGAR
¼ CUP MINCED FRESH DILL
2 TABLESPOONS UNSALTED
    BUTTER
2 TABLESPOONS LEMON JUICE
½ TEASPOON SALT
¼ TEASPOON FRESHLY
    GROUND PEPPER
6 LEMON SLICES
1-2 SPRIGS FRESH DILL

LEMON DILL RICE

In a saucepan combine rice and oil. Cook over medium heat, stirring often, until grains are light golden brown, about 4 minutes.

Add onion and celery, stirring often until they are softened, about 3 minutes. Add garlic and cook for 1 minute. Add chicken stock, sugar, dill, butter, lemon juice, salt and pepper. Heat to a boil, reduce heat to low and arrange lemon slices on top of rice.

Cover tightly and simmer gently until rice is tender and the liquid is absorbed, about 20 minutes. Let stand, covered, for 12 minutes. Garnish with dill. *Yield: 4 servings.*

½   CUP CHOPPED ONION
3   TABLESPOONS BUTTER
4   CUPS COOKED RICE
½   SMALL RED PEPPER,
      FINELY CHOPPED
½   SMALL GREEN PEPPER,
      FINELY CHOPPED
2   CUPS SOUR CREAM
1   CUP COTTAGE CHEESE
½   BAY LEAF, CRUSHED
      SALT AND FRESHLY GROUND
      PEPPER TO TASTE
4   OUNCES CHOPPED
      GREEN CHILIS
2½ CUPS GRATED
      LONGHORN CHEESE

RICE GUADALUPE

Preheat oven to 375° F. In a large saucepan sauté onion in butter until light brown. Add all remaining ingredients except ½ cup cheese. Mix well.

Place in greased 2-quart casserole. Cover and bake for 25 minutes. Remove from oven and sprinkle reserved cheese on top. Bake uncovered for an additional 10 minutes. *Yield: 10 servings.*

1   CUP PINE NUTS
5   CUPS WATER
1   CUP COCONUT MILK
4   SLICES BACON, DICED
½   CUP MINCED GREEN ONIONS
2   CLOVES GARLIC, MINCED
1   TEASPOON MINCED HOT PEPPER
1   TEASPOON SALT
1   TEASPOON THYME
¼   TEASPOON FRESHLY GROUND
      BLACK PEPPER
2   CUPS LONG-GRAIN WHITE RICE

RICE AND PINE NUTS

In a large saucepan combine pine nuts, water, coconut milk and bacon. Bring to a boil. Reduce heat to low, cover and simmer for 1½ hours.

Stir in onions, garlic, hot pepper, salt, thyme and freshly ground pepper. Bring to a boil. Stir in rice. Reduce heat to low, cover and simmer until rice is tender, about 20 minutes.

Season to taste. Fluff rice with fork and serve.
Yield: 6 to 8 servings.

VEGETABLES

The John Hancock Building, built in 1969, is a prominent landmark on Chicago's famous skyline. This 100-story tower rises more than 1,000 feet in the air and houses a combination of residential, commercial and retail tenants. An observation deck, open to the public, is located on the 94th floor.

1⅓	POUNDS FRESH THIN ASPARAGUS, PEELED AND TRIMMED
1	TABLESPOON RICE VINEGAR
1	TEASPOON SOY SAUCE
1	TEASPOON SESAME OIL
1	CLOVE GARLIC, MINCED
¼	TEASPOON MINCED GINGER ROOT
	DASH OF CHILI OIL

ASPARAGUS WITH CHINESE VINAIGRETTE

Blanch asparagus 3 minutes in boiling water. Rinse with cold water and pat dry. Place asparagus in a serving dish.

In a small bowl combine remaining ingredients. Pour over asparagus. Chill for 30 minutes. *Yield: 4 servings.*

1	POUND FRESH THIN ASPARAGUS, PEELED AND TRIMMED
1½	CUPS WHIPPING CREAM
3	EGGS, BEATEN
2	EGG YOLKS, BEATEN
¾	TEASPOON SALT
¼	TEASPOON FRESHLY GROUND PEPPER
	SEVERAL PINCHES NUTMEG
2	TABLESPOONS BUTTER, SOFTENED
4	SLICES OF PEELED ORANGE, CUT IN HALF, AS GARNISH
	ORANGE SAUCE
1	CUP PLUS 2 TABLESPOONS FRESHLY SQUEEZED
¼	CUP SUGAR
1	TABLESPOON LEMON JUICE
1	PINCH CREAM OF TARTAR
1	TEASPOON ARROWROOT

HOT ASPARAGUS MOUSSE WITH ORANGE SAUCE

Preheat oven to 400° F. Steam asparagus until very tender, about 7 minutes. Cut in pieces and place in a food processor. Purée about 2 minutes. With machine running, slowly add cream. Pour mixture through a strainer into a bowl, pressing until only fibers remain. Discard fibers. Add eggs, egg yolks, salt, pepper and nutmeg to asparagus purée. Stir well.

Butter six ½-cup ramekins. Divide asparagus mixture evenly among them. Place ramekins in a large pan filled with enough water to reach 1″ up the side of ramekins. Bake on lowest rack in oven until a knife inserted in center comes out clean, about 20-25 minutes. Keep warm in water bath until serving time.

For Orange Sauce, mix 1 cup of the orange juice, sugar and lemon juice in a saucepan and heat to boil. Mix cream of tartar and arrowroot with remaining 2 tablespoons orange juice and add to the saucepan. Cook until clear and slightly thickened.

Spoon 3-4 tablespoons Orange Sauce on warmed salad plates. Loosen asparagus mousse by running knife around edge of ramekins. Unmold onto center of plates. Garnish with orange slices. Serve immediately. *Yield: 4 servings.*

ASPARAGUS WITH RED PEPPER HOLLANDAISE

4	EGG YOLKS AT ROOM TEMPERATURE
¼	TEASPOON SALT
	WHITE PEPPER TO TASTE
1-2	TABLESPOONS FRESHLY SQUEEZED LEMON JUICE
2	TABLESPOONS BUTTER, MELTED
1	RED BELL PEPPER, ROASTED, PEELED AND PURÉED
2	POUNDS THIN ASPARAGUS, PEELED AND TRIMMED
	CHERVIL SPRIGS AS GARNISH

In a food processor blend egg yolks, salt, pepper and lemon juice. With motor running, pour in hot butter in a steady stream. Add pepper purée and blend. Pour into a nonaluminum bowl and keep warm in a water bath.

In a large saucepan of boiling water, cook asparagus until crisp-tender. Drain. Immediately immerse in ice water. Drain, pat dry and place on serving plate. Drizzle the Red Pepper Hollandaise in a thin ribbon across the asparagus and garnish with chervil sprigs. *Yield: 6 to 8 servings.*

SPICY INDIAN CABBAGE

1	HEAD CABBAGE, SHREDDED
½	TEASPOON FINELY CHOPPED FRESH GINGER
½	TEASPOON FINELY CHOPPED GREEN CHILI
2	TABLESPOONS VEGETABLE OIL
1	TABLESPOON MUSTARD SEED

Shred cabbage and squeeze out excess water. Place in a bowl and add ginger and chili.

In a large saucepan heat oil and add mustard seed. Cook until seed crackles. Add cabbage mixture and stir-fry until cabbage is tender, about 5 minutes. Serve immediately. *Yield: 6 servings.*

SPICY BROCCOLI WITH TOMATOES

6	CUPS BROCCOLI
2	PLUM TOMATOES, PEELED AND SEEDED
2	TABLESPOONS EXTRA VIRGIN OLIVE OIL
	PINCH OF DRIED, HOT RED PEPPER
1	CLOVE GARLIC, CRUSHED
	SALT AND FRESHLY GROUND PEPPER TO TASTE

Cut broccoli tops into bite-sized florets. Cut the stems into 1″ lengths. Steam broccoli until crisp-tender, about 4 minutes. Drain.

Cut tomatoes lengthwise into eighths. Set aside.

Heat oil in skillet and add the broccoli, red pepper, tomato, garlic, salt and pepper. Stir-fry until crisp-tender, about 2 minutes. Serve immediately. *Yield: 4 servings.*

3 EGGS, SEPARATED
4 TABLESPOONS SUGAR
1½ TABLESPOONS CORNSTARCH
1 CUP MILK
3 CUPS COOKED AND
    MASHED CARROTS
3 TABLESPOONS BUTTER
1 TEASPOON SALT
1 CUP BREAD CRUMBS
1 CUP HALF-AND-HALF
¾ TEASPOON GROUND NUTMEG
¼ CUP CREAM SHERRY

CARROT SOUFFLÉ

Beat egg yolks with sugar until light. Set aside.

Mix cornstarch with small amount of milk. In a large saucepan heat remaining milk. Add cornstarch mixture and stir until smooth and slightly thickened.

Stir small amount of cornstarch mixture into egg and sugar mixture. Stir to mix well. Pour mixture into hot milk, cooking and stirring over medium heat until smooth and thick. Remove from heat and set aside. *Preheat oven to 300° F.*

Add carrots, butter, salt and bread crumbs. Blend evenly.

Stir in half-and-half, nutmeg and sherry, mixing well.

Beat egg whites until stiff. Fold into carrot mixture. Pour mixture into 2-quart buttered soufflé dish.

Place soufflé dish in roasting pan with enough water to come ½″-1″ up the side of the soufflé dish. Bake 30 minutes.

Increase oven temperature to 350° F and continue baking 45 minutes or until a knife inserted in center comes out clean. Serve immediately. *Yield: 10 servings.*

4 CUPS COOKED DRIED
    WHITE BEANS
2 TABLESPOONS EXTRA VIRGIN
    OLIVE OIL
1 TABLESPOON LEMON JUICE
½ TABLESPOON CHOPPED
    FRESH BASIL
½ TABLESPOON CHOPPED
    FRESH PARSLEY
½ TABLESPOON CHOPPED
    FRESH ROSEMARY
½ TABLESPOON CHOPPED FRESH
    MARJORAM
½ CUP CHOPPED TOMATO
4 LEAVES RADICCHIO

SMALL WHITE BEANS WITH FRESH HERBS

In a medium bowl combine beans, olive oil and lemon juice. Just before serving, stir in herbs and tomato. Place one radicchio leaf on each plate and spoon beans on top. *Yield: 4 servings.*

1	OUNCE RAISINS
1	SMALL HEAD CAULIFLOWER, TRIMMED
¼	CUP EXTRA VIRGIN OLIVE OIL
2	TEASPOONS MINCED GARLIC
1	OUNCE PINE NUTS
	SALT AND FRESHLY GROUND PEPPER
2	TABLESPOONS CHOPPED PARSLEY

CAULIFLOWER WITH RAISINS AND PINE NUTS

Soak the raisins in water to cover for 15-20 minutes. Drain raisins and pat dry.

Place cauliflower into 4 quarts of boiling water. After the water returns to a boil, cook for 6-7 minutes until crisp-tender. Drain and cut into 1½″ pieces.

In a large sauté pan, over medium heat, add oil and garlic. Cook until garlic turns to a pale golden color.

Add the raisins, cauliflower, pine nuts, salt and pepper. Cover and reduce heat to low. Cook for 8-10 minutes, stirring occasionally, until the cauliflower is tender.

Sprinkle with chopped parsley and serve immediately.

Yield: 4 to 6 servings.

1¼	POUNDS FENNEL, TRIMMED AND COARSELY CHOPPED
2	TABLESPOONS UNSALTED BUTTER
1	MEDIUM ONION, FINELY CHOPPED
¼	CUP BEEF BROTH
2	MEDIUM TOMATOES, SEEDED AND CHOPPED
	PINCH OF FRESH THYME LEAVES
1½	TEASPOONS PERNOD
	SALT AND FRESHLY GROUND PEPPER
	FEATHERY LEAVES OF FENNEL AS GARNISH

BRAISED FENNEL

Parboil fennel in lightly salted water 2 minutes. Drain.

In a saucepan, over medium heat, melt butter and cook onion until translucent. Add fennel, broth, tomatoes and thyme. Reduce heat, cover and simmer 20 minutes.

Uncover and simmer until liquid has evaporated. Add Pernod, salt and pepper to taste. Serve garnished with fennel leaves.

Yield: 4 servings.

1	POUND SHELLED FRESH PEAS
½	POUND SUGAR SNAP PEAS, STRINGS REMOVED
⅓	POUND SNOW PEAS, STRINGS REMOVED
1	TABLESPOON BUTTER
2	TABLESPOONS WHIPPING CREAM SALT AND FRESHLY GROUND PEPPER

THREE PEA MÉLANGE

In a saucepan steam all peas until crisp-tender.

Drain, then toss with butter, cream, salt and pepper to taste. *Yield: 6 servings.*

2	RED BELL PEPPERS
2	YELLOW BELL PEPPERS
2	PEACH-COLORED BELL PEPPERS
5	TABLESPOONS BUTTER SALT AND FRESHLY GROUND PEPPER TO TASTE
3	LARGE EGGS
¾	CUP MILK
1	CUP WHIPPING CREAM
1	CUP GRATED GRUYÈRE CHEESE

COLORFUL GRUYÈRE CUSTARD

Preheat oven to 375° F. Grill peppers until blackened. Remove the skins and cut peppers into strips. Sauté briefly in butter, about 1 minute. Add salt and pepper to taste.

In a large bowl beat together eggs, milk and cream. Add pepper mixture. Pour into a buttered baking dish and sprinkle with Gruyère.

Bake for 25-30 minutes. Serve immediately. *Yield: 6 servings.*

6	SMALL JAPANESE EGGPLANTS
6	BELL PEPPERS: RED, YELLOW AND GREEN
1	CUP EXTRA VIRGIN OLIVE OIL SALT AND FRESHLY GROUND PEPPER

GRILLED PEPPERS AND EGGPLANT

Slice eggplants vertically to the stem, ¼″ thick, and fan out slices.

Stem, seed and quarter peppers.

Brush eggplant and peppers with oil and season with salt and pepper.

Grill a few minutes until each side is tender. *Yield: 6 servings.*

6	RED BELL PEPPERS
8	OUNCES PESTO
10	OUNCES GOAT CHEESE WITH GARLIC AND HERBS
3	TOMATOES, SLICED AND QUARTERED

PESTO PEPPERS WITH GOAT CHEESE

Preheat oven to 350° F. Remove stems from peppers. Cut off top ½" of peppers and reserve. Remove seeds and ribs from peppers.

Put 2 tablespoons of pesto into each pepper rotating to coat insides.

Cut goat cheese into 6 pieces. Place ¾ of each piece into each pepper.

Fill peppers with tomatoes.

Drizzle remaining pesto over the 6 stuffed peppers. Top with remaining goat cheese. Replace pepper tops.

In a baking pan stand peppers upright with sides touching. Carefully add ½ cup water to pan. Bake peppers 40 minutes. *Yield: 6 servings.*

40	SMALL, UNIFORM NEW POTATOES
1	SMALL EGGPLANT, PEELED, FINELY CHOPPED
1	RED BELL PEPPER, FINELY CHOPPED
1	GREEN BELL PEPPER, FINELY CHOPPED
1	YELLOW BELL PEPPER, FINELY CHOPPED
2	CLOVES GARLIC, MINCED
½	CUP FINELY CHOPPED BERMUDA ONION
1	CUP FINELY CHOPPED ZUCCHINI
2	LARGE, RIPE TOMATOES, FINELY CHOPPED
2	TABLESPOONS CHOPPED FRESH THYME
2	TABLESPOONS CHOPPED FRESH OREGANO
	SALT AND WHITE PEPPER
1	BUNCH FRESH CHIVES, CHOPPED

NEW POTATOES STUFFED WITH RATATOUILLE

Boil new potatoes until tender, about 15-20 minutes. Drain and cool. Cut evenly in half. Trim the bottoms so potatoes sit flat. Scoop out center of each potato with melon baller, keeping shell of potato intact. Chill shells.

On high heat sauté eggplant, peppers, garlic, onion and zucchini until tender. Add tomatoes, thyme and oregano. Remove from heat. Salt and pepper to taste. *Preheat oven to 300° F.*

Fill each potato shell with Ratatouille. Place in baking pan and bake until heated through, about 10-15 minutes. Sprinkle with chives. Serve immediately. *Yield: 40 stuffed potatoes.*

1 BUNCH DILL
4 BABY ARTICHOKES, TRIMMED
   AND WASHED
6 SMALL RED POTATOES, WASHED
1 LEMON
4 TABLESPOONS BUTTER, MELTED
   SALT AND FRESHLY
   GROUND PEPPER

STEAMED BABY ARTICHOKES AND RED POTATOES

In a large pot place ¾ of the dill on a steamer tray. Cover dill with vegetables. Halve the lemon and squeeze the juice over the vegetables. Cover tightly and steam until vegetables are tender, about 15-20 minutes.

Brush the vegetables with melted butter, garnish with remaining dill. Season to taste and serve immediately. *Yield: 2 servings.*

---

6 RIPE TOMATOES, PEELED
   AND CORED
8 OUNCES TOMATO SAUCE
2 TEASPOONS CURRY POWDER
1 TABLESPOON CURRANT JELLY
   SALT AND FRESHLY GROUND
   PEPPER TO TASTE
¼ CUP GRATED MILD
   CHEDDAR CHEESE
¼ CUP BUTTERED BREAD CRUMBS
6 SLICES BACON, COOKED
   AND CRUMBLED

BAKED CURRIED TOMATOES

Preheat oven to 375° F. Arrange tomatoes in a deep, buttered baking dish.

In a small saucepan, over medium heat, combine tomato sauce, curry powder and jelly. Cook 5 minutes. Add salt and pepper to taste. Pour mixture over tomatoes.

Combine cheese and bread crumbs. Sprinkle over tomatoes. Bake for 20 minutes until heated through. Serve topped with crumbled bacon. *Yield: 6 servings.*

---

1 9″ PIE SHELL, BAKED
   AND COOLED
6 MEDIUM TOMATOES,
   THINLY SLICED
3 SPRIGS FRESH BASIL
1 CUP GRATED CHEDDAR CHEESE
1 CUP MAYONNAISE

GARDEN TOMATO PIE

Preheat oven to 350° F. In the bottom of the pie shell place a layer of tomatoes.

Tear basil leaves into ¼″-½″ pieces. Sprinkle tomato layer with ⅓ of basil leaves. Continue layering tomatoes and basil until pie shell is full.

Combine cheese and mayonnaise. Spread on top of tomato and basil pie.

Bake for 40 minutes, until golden brown.

Let stand 15 minutes before serving. May be served cold. *Yield: 6 servings.*

2½	POUNDS MILD ITALIAN SAUSAGE, IN CASING
1	CUP WATER
3	TABLESPOONS EXTRA VIRGIN OLIVE OIL
6	SMALL NEW POTATOES, CUBED SALT AND FRESHLY GROUND PEPPER
3	MEDIUM GARLIC CLOVES, MINCED
2	MEDIUM RED ONIONS
3	MEDIUM BELL PEPPERS: RED, YELLOW AND GREEN
3	MEDIUM ZUCCHINI
3	MEDIUM YELLOW SQUASH
2	TABLESPOONS FRESHLY SQUEEZED LEMON JUICE
1	CUP CHOPPED FRESH BASIL LEAVES

VEGETABLE SAUSAGE RAGOUT

In a large pan, over medium heat, cook sausage in water about 12-15 minutes, until water evaporates. Add oil to pan with sausage and heat. When hot, add potatoes, salt and pepper. Reduce heat and simmer, turning sausage and stirring potatoes occasionally. Cook until sausage is well done and brown on all sides, about 11 minutes. Remove sausage and set aside.

Cut onion and peppers into ¾″ pieces. Add onions, peppers and garlic to potatoes and cook, uncovered, over medium heat until peppers are tender, about 7-8 minutes, stirring occasionally.

Slice zucchini and yellow squash into ⅜″ rounds. Add to vegetable mixture. Continue cooking until vegetables are crisp-tender, about 5 minutes longer.

Cut sausage into 1½″ pieces and add to the vegetable mixture along with lemon juice. Cook just until heated through, about 2 minutes. Remove from heat and add basil. Serve hot or at room temperature. *Yield: 8 servings.*

1	POUND FRESH ASPARAGUS, SLICED INTO 1½″ PIECES
1	YELLOW PEPPER, SEEDED AND CUT INTO 1½″ PIECES
½	POUND CARROTS, PEELED AND SLICED DIAGONALLY
1	TEASPOON GREEK SEASONING

TRI-COLOR VEGETABLES

Blanche all vegetables individually for 2 minutes.
Combine and sprinkle with seasoning.
Yield: 4 to 6 servings.

ORCHESTRA HALL is a fitting home to the world-renowned Chicago Symphony Orchestra. Designed by Daniel H. Burnham and built in 1905, the building derives its style from the Italian Renaissance. Built with Indiana limestone and red brick, the facade is decorated with the names of Bach, Mozart, Beethoven, Schumann and Wagner.

....

FILET MIGNON WITH MUSTARD GLAZE

4	FILETS MIGNON
4	TABLESPOONS HONEY MUSTARD
2	TABLESPOONS SOY SAUCE
2	CLOVES GARLIC, MINCED
1	TABLESPOON FRESH GINGER ROOT, MINCED
1	TABLESPOON CRUSHED, DRIED ROSEMARY

Preheat broiler. Broil meat on one side. While meat is cooking, mix together remaining ingredients for glaze.

Turn meat over, coat with glaze. Move to lower rack in oven and continue cooking until meat is done. Watch closely to make sure glaze doesn't burn.

Let stand 5 minutes before serving. *Yield: 4 servings.*

....

GARLIC-ROASTED CHATEAUBRIAND WITH COGNAC MUSTARD SAUCE

2	BEEF TENDERLOINS (2½ POUNDS EACH), TRIMMED
5	MEDIUM GARLIC CLOVES, VERY FINELY SLIVERED
2½	TABLESPOONS EXTRA VIRGIN OLIVE OIL
1½	TABLESPOONS UNSALTED BUTTER
	SALT AND FRESHLY GROUND PEPPER TO TASTE
	COGNAC MUSTARD SAUCE
1½	TABLESPOONS BUTTER
4	MEDIUM SHALLOTS, MINCED
2	CUPS BEEF STOCK
2	TABLESPOONS COGNAC
2	TABLESPOONS DIJON MUSTARD
½	CUP UNSALTED BUTTER, CUT INTO 8 PIECES
3	TABLESPOONS MINCED FRESH PARSLEY

Cut ¾″ deep slits in meat. Insert garlic slivers into slits. Brush meat with 2 tablespoons of the oil. Set aside.

Preheat oven to 450° F. In large skillet heat remaining oil over medium high heat. Add meat and brown on all sides. Remove meat to rack in roasting pan. Set skillet aside.

Roast meat to desired doneness, about 40 minutes for medium-rare.

For sauce, melt butter in reserved skillet. Add shallots and sauté until softened, about 4 minutes.

Remove tenderloins from roasting pan. Set aside. Skim fat from pan. Over high heat, stir in stock, scraping up browned bits. Add shallots. Bring to a boil and cook until reduced by half. Add cognac and boil 1 minute. Reduce heat to low. Whisk in mustard. Whisk in butter, 1 piece at a time. Cook until butter is melted. Stir in parsley. Season with salt and freshly ground pepper to taste.

Carve meat into ½″ slices. Spoon sauce over and serve immediately. *Yield: 8 servings.*

1	TOMATO, PEELED, SEEDED AND CHOPPED
½	POUND CREAM CHEESE, SOFTENED
1	TABLESPOON DIJON MUSTARD
½	CUP SLICED SCALLIONS
2	TABLESPOONS RED CAVIAR
½	POUND BUTTER, SOFTENED
2	POUNDS FLANK STEAK, POUNDED AND SCORED
½	CUP CHOPPED WATERCRESS AS GARNISH
6	CHERRY TOMATOES AS GARNISH

BEEF WITH CAVIAR BUTTER

In a saucepan, over low heat, cook tomato until thick and moisture is reduced. Set aside to cool.

Preheat broiler. In a food processor combine cream cheese, mustard, scallions, caviar, butter and cooked tomato. Process to mix.

Broil flank steak to desired doneness, 5-7 minutes each side for medium-rare.

Remove steak to a large serving platter. Spread caviar butter over steak. Roll up and secure with toothpicks. Slice.

Serve immediately, garnished with watercress and cherry tomatoes. *Yield: 6 servings.*

2	GARLIC CLOVES, MINCED
2	TABLESPOONS SOY SAUCE
2	TEASPOONS GRATED FRESH GINGER ROOT
3	TABLESPOONS FRESHLY SQUEEZED LEMON JUICE
1	POUND FLANK STEAK, CUT DIAGONALLY INTO NARROW STRIPS
2	TEASPOONS CORNSTARCH
⅓	CUP BEEF BROTH
1	TABLESPOON VEGETABLE OIL
2	CUPS QUARTERED FRESH MUSHROOMS
1½	CUPS SLICED ASPARAGUS, CUT DIAGONALLY INTO 1½″ PIECES
3	SCALLIONS, SLICED DIAGONALLY INTO 1″ PIECES

GINGERED BEEF WITH ASPARAGUS

In a bowl combine garlic, soy sauce, ginger root and lemon juice. Add beef and toss to coat. Remove beef and reserve marinade.

Dissolve cornstarch in broth. Set aside.

Preheat wok. Add oil. Stir-fry mushrooms and beef strips, over medium-high heat, until beef loses its red color, about 3 minutes. Add asparagus and scallions and continue to stir-fry until asparagus is crisp-tender. Stir in cornstarch mixture and reserved marinade. Cook until thickened. *Yield: 4 servings.*

10-12 POUND FULLY COOKED
       WHOLE HAM
⅓ CUP DIJON MUSTARD
½ CUP FIRMLY PACKED LIGHT
       BROWN SUGAR
½ CUP DRY SHERRY
1¾ CUPS FRESH BREAD CRUMBS
⅔ CUP FINELY GROUND PECANS
¾ CUP FRESH CHOPPED PARSLEY
      PARSLEY SPRIGS
      SHERRIED MUSTARD SAUCE
2 TABLESPOONS BUTTER
3 TABLESPOONS FLOUR
1½ CUPS CHICKEN BROTH
2 BAY LEAVES
1 CUP PLUS 2 TABLESPOONS
      DRY SHERRY
6 TABLESPOONS DIJON MUSTARD

BAKED HAM WITH SHERRIED MUSTARD SAUCE

Preheat oven to 325° F. Trim off ham rind and any fat to ¼″ thickness.

Place ham on rack in large roasting pan. Bake for 1½ hours. Remove from oven and score top of ham into 1″ squares. Brush with mustard and sprinkle with brown sugar. Return to oven and bake 1 hour. Remove from oven and set aside.

Combine sherry, bread crumbs, pecans and ¼ cup of the chopped parsley. Mix well. Gently pat crumb mixture onto ham leaving three 1″ strips open for parsley sprigs as garnish later.

Return ham to oven and bake for ½ hour. Garnish 1″ strips on ham with remaining ½ cup chopped parsley. Serve with Sherried Mustard Sauce.

For sauce, melt butter in a saucepan. Stir in flour to make a roux. Cook over medium heat, stirring constantly, for 1 minute. Gradually stir in broth, bay leaves and 6 tablespoons of the sherry and continue to cook until sauce thickens and is smooth. Lower the heat and simmer 5 minutes. In a separate saucepan heat remaining sherry until reduced by half. Stir in mustard. Gradually combine the 2 sherry mixtures. Cook over low heat 5 minutes. Remove bay leaves before serving. *Yield: 12 servings.*

1 POUND PORK
TENDERLOIN, TRIMMED
½ CUP FLOUR
½ POUND FRESH ASPARAGUS
SPEARS, TRIMMED
AND PEELED
2 TABLESPOONS BUTTER
4 THIN SLICES PROSCIUTTO
LEEK SAUCE
3 TABLESPOONS BUTTER
2 MEDIUM LEEKS, WHITE PART
ONLY, CLEANED, CHOPPED
1 CUP WHIPPING CREAM
1½ TABLESPOONS FRESHLY
GRATED HORSERADISH
2 TEASPOONS FRESHLY SQUEEZED
LEMON JUICE
¼ TEASPOON SALT
¼ TEASPOON FRESHLY
GROUND PEPPER

PORK TENDERLOIN ROLLS WITH LEEK SAUCE

Cut tenderloin into ¼″ thick slices. Pound each into thin 3″ circles. Lightly flour meat and set aside.

In a large pot bring water to a boil. Add asparagus and cook until crisp-tender, about 6 minutes. Rinse under cold water. Drain. Set aside on paper towel to dry.

For Leek Sauce, in a saucepan, over medium heat, melt butter. Add leeks. Sauté until limp but not brown. Add cream. Bring to a boil. Reduce heat and cook until slightly thickened. Add horse-radish, lemon juice, salt and pepper. Set aside.

In a large skillet, over medium heat, melt 2 tablespoons butter. Sauté pork, turning once, just until cooked through and no longer pink, about 4 minutes.

Remove pork to a platter. Lay a slice of prosciutto and a few spears of asparagus across the center of each pork circle. Roll the pork around the prosciutto and asparagus so that the asparagus shows at either end of the roll. Secure with a toothpick.

Pour warm leek sauce over pork and serve immediately.

Yield: 4 servings.

7 TABLESPOONS FRESHLY
  SQUEEZED LEMON JUICE
2 LARGE CLOVES GARLIC, MINCED
4 TABLESPOONS TOMATO SAUCE
¾ TEASPOON SALT
1½ POUNDS LEAN PORK, CUT INTO
  ¾″ CUBES
2 TABLESPOONS CREAMY
  PEANUT BUTTER
1 TABLESPOON BUTTER
½ TEASPOON SUGAR
½ TEASPOON HOT RED
  PEPPER SAUCE
¼ CUP HALF-AND-HALF

SKEWERED INDONESIAN SATE

Combine 6 tablespoons of the lemon juice, garlic, 3 tablespoons of the tomato sauce and salt. Pour over pork cubes and marinate in refrigerator for 3-4 hours, covered, turning occasionally.

Preheat broiler. Remove pork, reserving marinade, and thread meat on 4 skewers.

In a saucepan combine reserved marinade, remaining lemon juice, remaining tomato sauce, peanut butter, butter, sugar and pepper sauce over low heat. Stir constantly until thick. Remove from heat and gradually add half-and-half.

Broil the skewered meat, turning once, for 15 minutes or until done.

Serve immediately with warm sauce. *Yield: 4 servings.*

1¼ CUPS TOASTED HAZELNUTS
1 CUP DRIED BREAD CRUMBS
½ TEASPOON SALT
¼ TEASPOON FRESHLY GROUND
  PEPPER
1 POUND PORK TENDERLOIN
1 EGG MIXED WITH 1
  TABLESPOON WATER
3 TABLESPOONS VEGETABLE OIL
1 TABLESPOON FLOUR
⅓ CUP RUBY PORT WINE
1 TABLESPOON DIJON MUSTARD
  WITH SEEDS
½ CUP CHICKEN BROTH
½ CUP WATER
  WATERCRESS OR PARSLEY SPRIGS
  AS GARNISH

HAZELNUT-COATED PORK CUTLETS WITH PORT WINE SAUCE

Reserve a few whole nuts as garnish. In a food processor coarsely grind remaining nuts. Mix nuts, bread crumbs, salt and pepper and spread on waxed paper.

Cut pork tenderloin on a slant into ¼″ thick slices. Pound slices to ⅛″ thickness.

Dip slices into egg, then nut mixture to coat. Heat oil in a large skillet over medium heat. Cook pork slices until browned on both sides, 3-4 minutes. Remove pork to warm platter.

Stir flour into pan drippings in skillet over medium heat. Add port, mustard, broth and water. Stir to loosen brown bits from skillet. Cook until sauce boils and thickens slightly, stirring frequently.

Spoon sauce around pork slices on platter. Garnish with watercress and reserved whole nuts. *Yield: 4 servings.*

½ CUP SOY SAUCE
1 CUP FIRMLY PACKED LIGHT
   BROWN SUGAR
4 SCALLIONS, CHOPPED
   WITH TOPS
1 LIME, THINLY SLICED
   JUICE OF 1 LIME
2 TEASPOONS GRATED LIME PEEL
4 PORK CHOPS, 1½″ THICK
4 LIME SLICES AS GARNISH
2-4 TABLESPOONS WATER

ORIENTAL PORK CHOPS IN LIME MARINADE

In a large bowl combine soy sauce, sugar, scallions, lime, lime juice and lime peel.

Add chops and marinate in refrigerator for about 30 minutes.

Preheat oven to 325° F. Remove chops from marinade and reserve liquid. Brown chops very briefly in a non-stick skillet, over medium heat, being careful not to burn.

Remove chops from skillet and place in a shallow baking dish. Place remaining 4 lime slices on top.

Add water to the marinade. Pour over chops. Cover and bake about 45 minutes or until tender. *Yield: 4 servings.*

½ CUP DRY SHERRY
½ CUP LIGHT SOY SAUCE
3 CLOVES GARLIC,
   FINELY CHOPPED
¼ CUP FINELY GRATED, FRESH
   GINGER ROOT
2½ POUNDS SHOULDER OF LAMB

ORIENTAL SHOULDER OF LAMB

In a large nonaluminum bowl mix all ingredients except lamb. Add meat. Refrigerate, covered, turning lamb occasionally, for about 24 hours.

Prepare grill. Insert meat thermometer in lamb. Grill lamb in covered grill, basting with the marinade until the internal temperature of the lamb reaches 140-145° for medium-rare, about 1½ hours. *Yield: 6 servings.*

6 TABLESPOONS UNSALTED
  BUTTER
4 TABLESPOONS EXTRA VIRGIN
  OLIVE OIL
10 OUNCES FRESH SPINACH
  FRESHLY SQUEEZED
  LEMON JUICE
8 OUNCES WHOLE OR HALVED
  ARTICHOKE HEARTS
  SALT
3½-4 POUNDS BONELESS LOIN LAMB
  ROAST
2 MEDIUM CARROTS,
  THINLY SLICED
2 MEDIUM ONIONS,
  THINLY SLICED
  FRESHLY GROUND PEPPER
4 PARSLEY SPRIGS AND 1 BAY LEAF,
  TIED TOGETHER
1 TEASPOON FRESH THYME
1 CUP DRY WHITE WINE
  SAGE SAUCE
5 OR 6 SAGE LEAVES, MINCED
¼ CUP DRY WHITE WINE
32 OUNCES CHICKEN STOCK
1-2 TABLESPOONS CORNSTARCH OR
  ROUX OF BUTTER AND FLOUR
1 TEASPOON CHOPPED
  FRESH PARSLEY
2 TABLESPOONS BUTTER
  SALT AND FRESHLY
  GROUND PEPPER

LAMB ROAST STUFFED WITH SPINACH AND ARTICHOKES

Preheat oven to 325° F. To prepare the spinach, melt 2 tablespoons butter with 2 tablespoons oil in a large skillet over medium heat. Add spinach and sauté until wilted, 1-2 minutes. Set aside.

To prepare artichokes, melt 2 tablespoons butter in a skillet over medium heat. When the foam subsides, stir in 1 teaspoon lemon juice. Add the artichoke hearts and toss to coat. Season with salt. Set aside.

To stuff the roast, roll open the meat and lay flat. Place the spinach mixture and artichoke hearts on opposite sides of the roast, lengthwise. Carefully begin rolling from spinach side. When completely rolled, tie middle and ends securely with string.

In a large oven-proof pan, over medium-high heat, add remaining butter and oil. When oils begin to foam add the lamb. Brown it lightly on all sides. Remove meat and add the carrots and onions to the pan. Sauté vegetables for about 10 minutes or until the onions are wilted and the carrots are softened. Put meat back in the pan and sprinkle with salt and pepper. Add the herbs and white wine. Insert a meat thermometer into the roast. Place roast in oven and baste every 10 minutes. Roast until the thermometer reads 150-160°, depending on desired doneness, about 30-40 minutes.

Remove the roast to a warm platter. Strain the juice and skim off fat. Discard the parsley and bay leaf and press the onions and carrots through a strainer into the degreased juices. Simmer a few minutes and correct seasonings.

For Sage Sauce, reduce the sage and white wine until almost no liquid remains. Add sage reduction and chicken stock to degreased juices and reduce by one-half. Stir in cornstarch or roux to thicken slightly. Add parsley, butter, salt and pepper to taste. Serve over slices of lamb roast. *Yield: 4 to 6 servings.*

1	TABLESPOON DRY MUSTARD
1	TABLESPOON FRESHLY SQUEEZED LEMON JUICE
2	TEASPOONS SALT
1	TEASPOON FRESH THYME LEAVES
1	TEASPOON FRESH ROSEMARY LEAVES
1	TEASPOON FRESH MARJORAM LEAVES
¼	TEASPOON FRESHLY GROUND PEPPER
1	CLOVE GARLIC, MINCED
6-8	POUND LEG OF LAMB, BONED, NOT TIED
1	POUND PORK TENDERLOIN
¼	CUP WATER
2	TABLESPOONS FLOUR

PORK-STUFFED LEG OF LAMB

Preheat oven to 325° F. In a small bowl mix mustard, lemon juice, salt, thyme, rosemary, marjoram, pepper and garlic. Brush mixture inside leg of lamb.

Place tenderloin inside lamb. Wrap lamb around tenderloin and tie securely.

Insert meat thermometer so tip is in center of pork tenderloin. Place meat on rack in open shallow roasting pan. Do not cover. Roast until thermometer registers 170°, approximately 2½-3½ hours.

Remove roast from oven. Skim off excess fat. Add enough water to meat juices to measure 1¾ cups. Combine ¼ cup water and flour in a container with tightly fitting lid. Shake vigorously. Stir into drippings. Heat to a boil, stirring constantly. Boil 1 minute. Serve immediately. *Yield: 10 servings.*

6	SMALL LAMB SHANKS
	SALT AND FRESHLY GROUND PEPPER
1½	TABLESPOONS FLOUR
3	TABLESPOONS EXTRA VIRGIN OLIVE OIL
9	LARGE CLOVES GARLIC, THINLY SLICED
2	CUPS CHICKEN STOCK
1	CELERY STALK, CHOPPED
1	BAY LEAF
1½	CUPS DRY WHITE WINE
3	TEASPOONS CHOPPED FRESH OREGANO

SWEET GARLIC LAMB SHANKS

Trim fat from lamb shanks. Season with salt and pepper. Coat with flour.

In a large pan heat oil. Add lamb and brown on all sides. Drain fat. Add garlic, stock, celery, bay leaf, wine and oregano. Cover and bring to a boil. Reduce heat to simmer and cook gently for 1½ hours.

Remove shanks from pan. Skim fat and remove bay leaf from sauce. Serve immediately. *Yield: 6 servings.*

¼-½ POUND DRIED APRICOTS
½ CUP CALVADOS
½ CUP CHOPPED ONION
4 TABLESPOONS CHOPPED
 PARSLEY
1 TABLESPOON BUTTER
½ CUP PISTACHIO NUTS, SHELLED
4 POUNDS BONELESS,
 ROLLED VEAL
¼ CUP HONEY
½ CUP DRY WHITE WINE
 JUICE OF ½ LEMON

VEAL ROLL WITH APRICOTS IN CALVADOS

In a small bowl, soak apricots in Calvados for 2 hours. Add more Calvados if totally absorbed. Remove apricots with slotted spoon, reserving brandy.

Preheat oven to 325° F. Sauté apricots, onion and parsley in butter until onion is transparent. Add pistachio nuts and sauté for another minute. Remove from heat and set aside.

Untie roast and spread open until flat. Spread sautéed mixture on veal, leaving ½″ uncovered on all edges. Re-roll and re-tie roast. Insert meat thermometer.

Place roast in covered baking dish and cook 45 minutes, basting every 10-15 minutes with mixture of honey, wine, lemon juice and any leftover Calvados. Uncover roast and continue basting and roasting for another 30 minutes or until meat thermometer registers 160-165°. *Yield: 6 servings.*

4 4-OUNCE BONELESS
 VEAL CUTLETS
½ CUP FLOUR
4 TABLESPOONS BUTTER
 LEMON SLICES AS GARNISH
2 TABLESPOONS FINELY CHOPPED
 FRESH CHIVES AS GARNISH
 PARSLEY AS GARNISH
 MUSTARD CRABMEAT SAUCE
2 CUPS WHIPPING CREAM
3 TABLESPOONS COARSELY
 GROUND DIJON MUSTARD
1 TABLESPOON PREPARED
 HORSERADISH
6 OUNCES LUMP CRABMEAT
 SALT AND FRESHLY GROUND
 PEPPER TO TASTE

VEAL WITH MUSTARD CRABMEAT SAUCE

Pound each cutlet between sheets of plastic wrap to ⅛″ thickness. Flour cutlets lightly.

For sauce, put cream into medium saucepan. Simmer gently over low heat for about 10 minutes or until cream has reduced to 1 cup. Stir in mustard, horseradish, crabmeat, salt and pepper. Set aside, covered.

In a heavy skillet, melt butter over medium heat. Add cutlets. Sauté about 15 seconds on each side. Remove veal to warm plates.

Spoon sauce over veal and serve garnished with lemon, chives and parsley. *Yield: 4 servings.*

1½	POUNDS VEAL CUTLETS, THINLY SLICED
½	CUP FLOUR
	SALT AND FRESHLY GROUND PEPPER TO TASTE
¼	CUP EXTRA VIRGIN OLIVE OIL
½	CUP BUTTER
1	CLOVE GARLIC, MINCED
1	CUP SLICED FRESH MUSHROOMS
2	TABLESPOONS FLOUR
¼	CUP ROSÉ WINE

VEAL SCALLOPINE ROSÉ

Pound veal cutlets to ⅛″ thickness. Dredge in flour with salt and pepper.

In a skillet, over medium heat, combine oil and ¼ cup of the butter. Add garlic and veal and sauté until lightly browned. Remove cutlets from pan and set aside.

Add mushrooms and remaining ¼ cup butter to skillet. Cook over low heat. Stir in flour. Cook 1 minute, stirring constantly. Remove from heat. Gradually add wine, stirring constantly. Return to heat and stir until thickened.

Add cutlets to mushroom mixture and simmer, covered, until thoroughly heated. *Yield: 4 servings.*

4	OUNCES DRY VERMOUTH
1	OUNCE DRY WHITE WINE
1	TABLESPOON CHOPPED CHERVIL
1½	POUND FILET OR LOIN OF VEAL
	SALT AND FRESHLY GROUND PEPPER TO TASTE
2	TABLESPOONS BUTTER
	BASIL SAUCE
½	CUP WHIPPING CREAM
2	TABLESPOONS DRY WHITE WINE
2	TABLESPOONS ANISETTE-FLAVORED LIQUEUR
2	TABLESPOONS BUTTER
¼	CUP BEEF BROTH
2	TABLESPOONS FRESH BASIL

VERMOUTH MARINATED VEAL MEDALLIONS WITH BASIL SAUCE

In a bowl combine vermouth, wine and chervil. Add veal and marinate in refrigerator overnight, turning occasionally.

Remove veal from marinade and cut diagonally in thin slices. Set aside.

In a saucepan combine all sauce ingredients and bring to a boil. Remove immediately and cover.

In a large saucepan, sauté veal in butter until lightly browned. Arrange on platter and top with Basil Sauce. *Yield: 4 servings.*

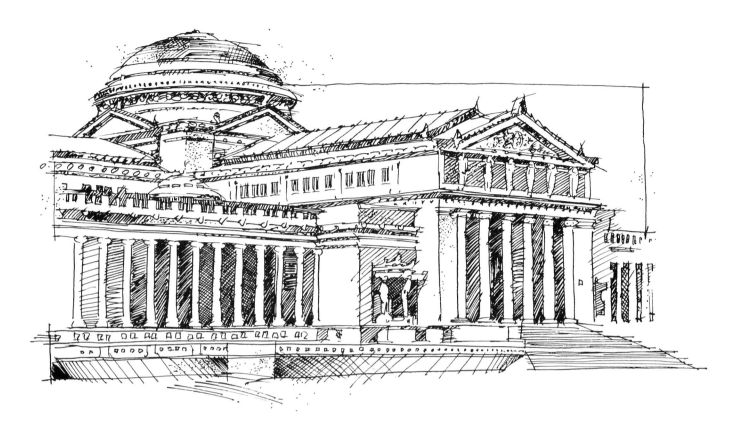

THE MUSEUM OF SCIENCE AND INDUSTRY was designed by Daniel H. Burnham and originally served as the Palace of Fine Arts for the 1893 Columbian Exposition. Designed in Greek Revivalist style, portions of its facade exactly duplicate parts of the Acropolis, Erechtheum and the Parthenon. Restoration and conversion of the building into a museum began in 1929 and continued until 1940.

4 OUNCES BUTTER

4 CHICKEN BREASTS, SPLIT,
   BONED AND SKINNED

1 CLOVE GARLIC, MINCED

½ POUND MUSHROOMS, SLICED

2 TABLESPOONS FRESHLY
   SQUEEZED LEMON JUICE

2 TABLESPOONS CAPERS, DRAINED
   DASH HOT RED PEPPER SAUCE

½ TEASPOON FRESHLY
   GROUND PEPPER

CHICKEN WITH LEMON CAPER SAUCE

In a large saucepan melt butter. Sauté chicken breasts, turning until lightly browned, about 5-8 minutes. Remove chicken and set aside.

In same saucepan add garlic and mushrooms and sauté until mushrooms are tender, about 4-5 minutes. Stir in lemon juice, capers, red pepper sauce and pepper. Simmer until sauce thickens. Return chicken to saucepan and continue simmering until warmed. *Yield: 4 to 6 servings.*

6 CHICKEN BREASTS, SPLIT,
   BONED AND SKINNED

½ TEASPOON SALT

½ TEASPOON FRESHLY
   GROUND PEPPER

⅓ CUP VEGETABLE OIL
   PARSLEY AS GARNISH
   LIME BUTTER SAUCE

8 TABLESPOONS BUTTER
   JUICE AND GRATED PEEL OF
   ONE LIME

1 TEASPOON MINCED
   FRESH CHIVES

1 TEASPOON MINCED FRESH
   DILL WEED

CHICKEN WITH LIME BUTTER SAUCE

Season chicken breasts with salt and pepper. In a large saucepan add oil and sauté chicken over medium heat for 4 minutes, until lightly brown. Turn chicken, cover and reduce heat to low. Simmer 10 minutes. Remove chicken and keep it warm.

For Lime Butter Sauce, in saucepan combine butter, lime juice and peel and cook until it begins to bubble. Reduce heat to low and stir until sauce is opaque and thick. Stir in chives and dill weed. Pour sauce over warm chicken and serve with parsley. *Yield: 6 servings.*

¼ CUP SOY SAUCE
2 TABLESPOONS BUTTER, MELTED
1 TABLESPOON CURRY POWDER
1 TEASPOON CINNAMON
1 TEASPOON GROUND GINGER
1 GARLIC CLOVE, CRUSHED
2 DASHES HOT RED PEPPER SAUCE
2 SMALL BROILER CHICKENS, SPLIT
  SESAME SEEDS

FORBIDDEN CITY CHICKEN

In a bowl mix together all ingredients except chicken and sesame seeds. Spread mixture over chicken and chill for 1 hour.

Preheat oven to 325° F. Sprinkle sesame seeds over chicken and bake for about 1 hour until chicken is golden. *Yield: 4 servings.*

2 WHOLE CHICKEN BREASTS,
    SKINNED AND BONED
2 TEASPOONS CORNSTARCH
3 TABLESPOONS SOY SAUCE
2 TABLESPOONS DRY SHERRY
1 TEASPOON GRATED FRESH
    GINGER ROOT
1 TEASPOON SUGAR
½ TEASPOON SALT
½ TEASPOON DRIED CRUSHED
    RED PEPPER
2 TABLESPOONS VEGETABLE OIL
2 MEDIUM GREEN PEPPERS, CUT
    INTO ¾" PIECES
4 SCALLIONS, SLICED DIAGONALLY
    INTO 1" PIECES
1 CUP WALNUT HALVES
3 CUPS COOKED RICE

GREEN PEPPER CHICKEN WITH WALNUTS

Cut chicken into 1" pieces and set aside. Stir together cornstarch and soy sauce. Add sherry, ginger root, sugar, salt and red pepper. Set aside.

Set wok over high heat. Add oil. To hot oil add green peppers and scallions. Stir-fry 2 minutes or until crisp-tender. Remove with a slotted spoon and set aside.

Add walnuts to wok. Stir-fry 1-2 minutes until golden. Remove from skillet with a slotted spoon and set aside. Stir-fry the chicken for 2 minutes. Add soy sauce mixture to chicken, stirring until thickened and bubbly. Stir in vegetables and walnuts. Cover and cook 1 minute more. Serve immediately with rice. *Yield: 6 servings.*

1	POUND FRESH APRICOTS, HALVED AND PITTED
3	TABLESPOONS BUTTER
¼	CUP FINELY CHOPPED ONION
1	CLOVE GARLIC, CRUSHED
½	TEASPOON DRY MUSTARD
1	TABLESPOON SOY SAUCE
⅛	TEASPOON SALT
¼	CUP FIRMLY PACKED LIGHT BROWN SUGAR
1	TEASPOON FRESHLY SQUEEZED LEMON JUICE
1	LARGE BROILER CHICKEN, CUT UP

GRILLED ORIENTAL CHICKEN WITH APRICOTS

Prepare charcoal grill. In a food processor purée half of the apricots.

Melt butter in small saucepan and add onion and garlic. Sauté until golden brown. Stir in mustard, soy sauce, salt, sugar, lemon juice and puréed apricots. Cook, stirring constantly, until mixture begins to simmer. Remove from heat.

Grill chicken over slow coals until almost cooked, about 35-45 minutes.

Put reserved apricots on a piece of heavy-duty foil. Place on grill. Brush chicken and apricots with sauce. Continue grilling, turning often and brushing with sauce, until golden, about 4 minutes.

Serve immediately surrounded by apricot halves.

Yield: 4 servings.

4	TABLESPOONS VEGETABLE OIL
2	GREEN ONIONS, SLICED DIAGONALLY INTO SMALL PIECES
2	CLOVES GARLIC, COARSELY CHOPPED
½	CUP UNSALTED WALNUTS
1	WHOLE CHICKEN BREAST, BONED, SKINNED, CUT INTO 1″ PIECES
1	TABLESPOON SOY SAUCE
½	POUND EGGPLANT, CUT IN 1½″ CUBES
½	CUP MARINATED ARTICHOKE HEARTS
2	TABLESPOONS HOISIN SAUCE
1	TABLESPOON FRESHLY SQUEEZED LEMON JUICE
½	CUP CHICKEN BROTH
2	TEASPOONS CORNSTARCH MIXED WITH 1 TABLESPOON BROTH

CHICKEN STIR-FRY WITH EGGPLANT AND ARTICHOKES

In a wok heat 2 tablespoons of the oil. When very hot add onions, garlic and nuts and stir-fry for 30 seconds. Transfer to a large bowl and set aside.

Add 1 tablespoon of the oil to the wok. Heat until very hot, add the chicken and stir-fry until browned on all sides, about 2 minutes. Season with ½ tablespoon of the soy sauce. Add to the nut mixture.

Add remaining tablespoon oil to the wok. When hot, add the eggplant. Stir-fry until well coated. Season with remaining ½ table-spoon soy sauce. Lower heat to medium, cover wok and cook just until tender, about 3 minutes.

Return chicken mixture and any juices to wok. Add artichoke hearts, hoisin, lemon juice and broth. Stir together until artichokes are warm. Taste and adjust seasonings. Add cornstarch mixture and stir until sauce thickens. Serve immediately. *Yield: 2 servings.*

CHICKEN BREASTS WITH SAGA BLUE CHEESE

4	CHICKEN BREASTS, SPLIT, BONED AND SKINNED
	SALT AND FRESHLY GROUND PEPPER
3	TABLESPOONS BUTTER
1	TABLESPOON FLOUR
½	CUP CHICKEN BROTH
¾	CUP HALF-AND-HALF
¼	POUND SAGA BLUE CHEESE, RIND REMOVED, CUT INTO PIECES
4	SLICES COOKED HAM
¼	CUP FINELY CHOPPED SHALLOTS
¼	CUP DRY VERMOUTH

Season chicken with salt and pepper.

Heat 2 tablespoons of the butter in a large skillet over medium-high heat. Add chicken and cook until lightly browned on one side. Turn and continue to cook about 5 minutes or until cooked through. Remove chicken and keep warm.

In a small saucepan melt remaining butter. Whisk in flour. Add broth and half-and-half, stirring rapidly. Cook 5 minutes. Add cheese, stirring until melted. Set aside.

Add ham slices to first skillet and cook briefly on both sides. Transfer ham to a heated serving dish and cover each slice with a chicken breast.

Add shallots to skillet and cook until wilted. Add the vermouth and stir, dissolving brown pieces. Stir in cheese sauce.

Strain sauce through a sieve into a small saucepan.

Pour sauce over chicken and serve immediately.

Yield: 4 servings.

KIWI POULET AU FRAMBOISE

2	SMALL BROILER CHICKENS, SPLIT
	SALT AND FRESHLY GROUND PEPPER
4	TABLESPOONS BUTTER, MELTED
8	OUNCES RASPBERRY PRESERVES
½	CUP DRY VERMOUTH
	GRATED PEEL OF 1 LARGE LEMON
2	KIWI FRUIT, PEELED AND SLICED

Preheat oven to 400° F. Season chicken with salt and pepper. Place chicken, skin side up, in a shallow roasting pan. Brush with butter. Bake for approximately 40 minutes or until tender.

In a small saucepan mix preserves, vermouth and lemon peel. Simmer for 2-3 minutes. Spoon glaze over cooked chicken. Top with kiwi slices and return to oven for 3-4 minutes. *Yield: 4 servings.*

2	CUPS RUBY PORT
½	CUP RED WINE VINEGAR
¼	CUP EXTRA VIRGIN OLIVE OIL
1	TEASPOON CORIANDER SEEDS
1	TEASPOON FENNEL SEEDS
2	TEASPOONS DRIED JUNIPER BERRIES
1	TEASPOON CRACKED BLACK PEPPERCORNS
2	GREEN ONIONS, CHOPPED
3	GARLIC CLOVES, CRUSHED
1	TABLESPOON MINCED FRESH GINGER ROOT
4	ROCK CORNISH GAME HENS

JUNIPER BERRY GAME BIRDS

In a nonaluminum bowl combine port, vinegar and oil.

In a grinder combine coriander, fennel, juniper berries and peppercorns and grind coarsely. Add to the port mixture with onions, garlic and ginger. Mix well.

Marinate the hens in the port mixture overnight in refrigerator. Turn the birds frequently in the marinade. Remove birds from the refrigerator ½ hour before grilling.

Prepare charcoal grill.

Remove birds from marinade and grill over a moderate fire until juices run clear when pierced near the joints with a fork, about 1¼ hours. *Yield: 4 servings.*

¾	CUP FRESHLY SQUEEZED ORANGE JUICE
¼	POUND DRIED PEACHES, THINLY SLICED
2	TABLESPOONS GRATED FRESH GINGER ROOT
1	TABLESPOON SOY SAUCE
1	TABLESPOON SAFFLOWER OIL
1	SCALLION, FINELY SLICED
2	TABLESPOONS BROWN SUGAR
2	TABLESPOONS FRESHLY SQUEEZED LIME JUICE
2	ROCK CORNISH GAME HENS, HALVED, BACKBONE REMOVED
½	TEASPOON SALT

PEACH-GLAZED CORNISH HENS WITH GINGER

Preheat broiler. In a small saucepan, over medium heat, combine orange juice, peaches, ginger, soy sauce, oil, scallion, brown sugar and lime juice. Cook, stirring once, for 5 minutes. Set aside.

Sprinkle the hens with the salt and place them on a broiler pan, skin side up. Broil until light brown, about 4 minutes.

Remove the hens from the broiler, discard the fat and *reduce oven temperature to 375° F.* Coat the hens with the peach glaze and bake for 30 minutes. *Yield: 4 servings.*

CHAMPAGNE ROASTED CORNISH HENS

4	ROCK CORNISH GAME HENS
	SALT AND FRESHLY
	GROUND PEPPER
4	TABLESPOONS MELTED BUTTER
1	CUP CHAMPAGNE
½	CUP WHIPPING CREAM
	FRESH WATERCRESS AS GARNISH

Preheat oven to 500° F. Season hens' cavities with salt and pepper. Fold wing tips under hens. Tie legs together. Brush melted butter on hens to completely cover. Place in open roasting pan. Roast for 10 minutes.

Reduce heat to 400° F. Pour champagne over hens. Continue roasting, basting frequently with pan juices, 30 minutes or until hens' juices run clear when pierced with a fork. Remove hens to serving platter. Keep warm.

Bring pan juices to a boil. Reduce heat to simmer and cook about 3-4 minutes. Add cream and heat through. Pour sauce over hens. Garnish with watercress. *Yield: 4 servings.*

PECAN STUFFED CORNISH HENS

8	TABLESPOONS BUTTER AT
	ROOM TEMPERATURE
½	CUP FINELY GROUND
	PECAN MEATS
1	TABLESPOON COGNAC
2	TABLESPOONS DIJON MUSTARD
	SALT AND FRESHLY
	GROUND PEPPER
2	ROCK CORNISH GAME HENS
2	TABLESPOONS VEGETABLE OIL
	SPRIGS OF PARSLEY AS GARNISH

Preheat oven to 450° F. In a bowl place 6 tablespoons of the butter, pecans, cognac, mustard, salt and pepper and blend well.

Pull the skin of each hen away from the body slightly and make a deep cavity to hold stuffing. Stuff each hen with pecan mixture. Truss hens.

Sprinkle the hens with salt and pepper. Arrange the hens breast side up on a baking dish. Brush with oil and bake for about 1 hour or until golden brown. Garnish with sprigs of parsley. *Yield: 4 servings.*

1	4½-POUND FRESH DUCK
3	TABLESPOONS VODKA
1	TEASPOON HOT RED PEPPER SAUCE
1	TABLESPOON WORCESTERSHIRE SAUCE
2	TABLESPOONS SOY SAUCE JUICE OF ONE LEMON
1	CLOVE GARLIC
2¼	TEASPOONS FRESH ROSEMARY
14	FRESH JUNIPER BERRIES, CRUSHED

ITALIAN GRILLED DUCK

Clean cavity of duck, cut off wing tips and remove excess fat. Wash and pat dry. Place duck in a shallow baking pan.

In a bowl combine remaining ingredients and rub the mixture over the duck. Place 4 tablespoons marinade in the duck cavity. Leave duck at room temperature for 1½-2 hours.

Preheat oven to 350° F. Before cooking, pierce duck with a sharp knife in several locations.

Place duck on a rack in a roasting pan and bake for 1 hour, basting twice. Allow to cool.

Prepare charcoal grill and set rack 6″ above coals.

Cut duck in half and remove backbone and rib bones. Place duck halves over rack. Grill for 20 minutes, basting with remaining marinade and turning once or twice. *Yield: 2 to 3 servings.*

4	TURKEY BREAST TENDERLOIN STEAKS
3	TABLESPOONS BUTTER, MELTED
1	LARGE ONION, CHOPPED
1	MEDIUM CARROT, CHOPPED
½	CUP SLICED MUSHROOMS
1½	TEASPOONS CHOPPED FRESH THYME
⅛	TEASPOON CAYENNE PEPPER
¼	TEASPOON SALT
1	TABLESPOON CHOPPED PARSLEY
2	MEDIUM ZUCCHINI, COARSELY SHREDDED FRESH THYME SPRIGS AS GARNISH

GRILLED TURKEY WITH THYME ON ZUCCHINI BED

Prepare charcoal grill. Grill turkey breasts over medium coals 20-25 minutes or until tender, turning once and brushing with melted butter.

In a medium saucepan sauté onion, carrot, mushrooms, thyme, cayenne and salt with the remaining hot butter. Cover and cook over low heat, 5-10 minutes or until vegetables are just tender. Stir in parsley.

Divide zucchini among 4 plates. Place turkey on zucchini bed and spoon vegetable mixture on top. Garnish with fresh thyme sprigs. *Yield: 4 servings.*

4	CUPS APPLE OR CHERRY WOOD CHIPS
¼	CUP CHOPPED HAZELNUTS, TOASTED
1	EGG YOLK
1	CUP LIGHTLY PACKED FRESH SPINACH LEAVES
1	CUP LIGHTLY PACKED FRESH BASIL LEAVES
1	TABLESPOON HAZELNUT OIL
1	CLOVE GARLIC, MINCED
¼	CUP FRESHLY GRATED PARMESAN CHEESE
½	FRESH TURKEY BREAST HALF, ABOUT 2½ POUNDS VEGETABLE OIL

HAZELNUT PESTO TURKEY BREAST

At least ½ hour before grilling, soak wood chips in enough water to cover. *Prepare charcoal grill.*

To make pesto, in a food processor blend hazelnuts until very finely chopped. Add egg yolk, spinach, basil, oil and garlic. Process until smooth. Stir in cheese and set aside.

Slip fingers under turkey skin to loosen it from meat, leaving skin attached at one edge. Spread pesto under the skin. Fold skin over pesto. Insert a meat thermometer in the thickest portion of the turkey breast.

In a covered grill arrange preheated coals around a drip pan. Sprinkle half of the drained wood chips on top of the preheated coals. To maintain the medium-hot coals throughout the cooking time, add 7 new coals to the grill every 25 minutes. Pour 1″ of water into drip pan.

Place breast, stuffed side up, on grill rack over drip pan but not over coals. Brush skin with oil. Cover grill. Grill breast to 170° F, about 1½ hours. Add remaining wood chips after 30 minutes. Add more water to drip pan as necessary. *Yield: 6 to 8 servings.*

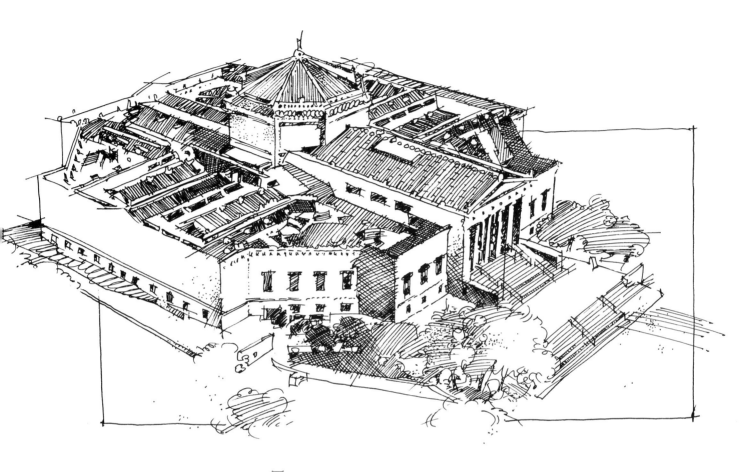

THE JOHN G. SHEDD AQUARIUM, built in 1929, is a solid example of the neoclassical Doric style common in many Chicago landmarks. John G. Shedd was a former chairman of Marshall Field & Co. The aquarium is one of the world's largest buildings devoted exclusively to living marine and freshwater aquatic life. It has more than 130 tanks displaying over 7,500 creatures, which represent more than 350 species.

20	MUSHROOMS, THINLY SLICED
4	HALIBUT FILLETS
	SALT AND FRESHLY
	GROUND PEPPER
⅔	CUP TOMATOES, PEELED,
	SEEDED AND CHOPPED
4	TABLESPOONS BUTTER
16	SPRIGS FRESH TARRAGON
4	TABLESPOONS DRY WHITE WINE

HALIBUT EN PAPILLOTE

Prepare charcoal grill. Cut a sheet of heavy-duty foil 15″ square. Arrange mushrooms in bed to one side.

If fillets are more than ¾″ thick, place between 2 sheets of waxed paper and pound lightly.

Lay fish on top of mushrooms and season with salt and pepper. Arrange tomatoes on top, then butter, then herbs. Sprinkle with wine. Fold foil over and seal edges tightly.

Grill fish for 9-10 minutes. Serve immediately.
Yield: 4 servings.

6	OUNCES SMOKED SALMON
2	EGG WHITES
1	TABLESPOON PARSLEY
¾	CUP WHIPPING CREAM
	SALT AND FRESHLY
	GROUND PEPPER
4	HALIBUT FILLETS
1	CUP CLAM BROTH, HEATED
½	CUP DRY WHITE WINE

HALIBUT WITH SMOKED SALMON MOUSSE

Preheat oven to 350° F. In a food processor chop salmon. Add 1 egg white and process for 30 seconds. Add second egg white and process for 10 seconds. Add parsley and chill 15 minutes. Add cream and process until smooth. Add salt and pepper to taste and pulse 6 times.

Place fillets in a buttered baking dish. Spread fillets with mousse. Pour hot broth and wine around fish. Cover with buttered parchment paper and bake until mousse is set and fish is cooked, about 15 minutes. *Yield: 4 servings.*

4	RED SNAPPER FILLETS
	SALT AND FRESHLY
	GROUND PEPPER
½	CUP MACADAMIA NUTS,
	FINELY GROUND
4	TABLESPOONS VEGETABLE OIL
4	TABLESPOONS PLUS 2
	TEASPOONS BUTTER
⅓	CUP CAPERS, DRAINED
1	TABLESPOON FRESHLY
	SQUEEZED LEMON JUICE
2	TABLESPOONS FINELY
	CHOPPED PARSLEY

MACADAMIA NUT RED SNAPPER

Season fish with salt and pepper. Coat fish on both sides with nuts.

In a large skillet heat oil and 2 teaspoons of the butter. Add the fillets and cook until golden brown on one side, about 3-4 minutes, basting fish as it cooks. Turn pieces and cook 2-3 minutes. Transfer fish to a warm platter.

Heat remaining butter in a small skillet. When it starts to brown, add capers and cook over high heat, shaking skillet and stirring, about 1 minute. Add lemon juice and pour mixture over the fish. Sprinkle with parsley and serve immediately. *Yield: 4 servings.*

¼	CUP WALNUT OIL
¼	CUP FRESHLY SQUEEZED
	LEMON JUICE
2	TEASPOONS CHOPPED
	FRESH ROSEMARY
	SALT AND FRESHLY
	GROUND PEPPER
12	FRESH JUMBO SHRIMP, PEELED,
	WITH TAILS
12	SEA SCALLOPS
1½	POUNDS FRESH TUNA, CUT IN
	1½″ PIECES
	ARUGULA BUTTER
1	CLOVE GARLIC
6	TABLESPOONS UNSALTED
	BUTTER, CHILLED, CUT
	IN PIECES
¾	CUP ARUGULA LEAVES
2	TABLESPOONS ITALIAN PARSLEY
½	TEASPOON FRESHLY SQUEEZED
	LEMON JUICE
¼	TEASPOON GREEN
	PEPPERCORNS
	SALT AND FRESHLY
	GROUND PEPPER

LAKESIDE GRILL WITH ARUGULA BUTTER

In a large bowl combine oil, lemon juice, rosemary, salt and pepper. Add seafood, seal tightly and chill for at least 4 hours. *Prepare charcoal grill.*

For Arugula Butter, in a food processor mince garlic. Add remaining ingredients and process until smooth.

Remove seafood from marinade and arrange on 6 skewers, alternating each item. Leave a small space between each piece so they cook evenly.

Grill skewers, turning once, just until fish turns opaque. Do not overcook. Spread each skewer with 1 tablespoon of softened Arugula Butter and serve immediately. *Yield: 6 servings.*

3 TABLESPOONS TARRAGON
 VINEGAR
1 MEDIUM ONION, HALVED
1 TEASPOON SALT
1 TEASPOON PEPPERCORNS
1 STALK CELERY, HALVED
6 SPRIGS FRESH PARSLEY
6 MAHI MAHI STEAKS
 EGG SAUCE
3 TABLESPOONS BUTTER
3 TABLESPOONS FLOUR
1 CUP RESERVED FISH STOCK
1 CUP WHIPPING CREAM
2 EGG YOLKS
2 HARD-COOKED EGGS,
 COARSELY CHOPPED
2 TABLESPOONS CHOPPED
 PARSLEY

POACHED MAHI MAHI WITH EGG SAUCE

In a large poaching pan combine all ingredients except egg sauce. Add enough water to cover fish. Bring to a gentle boil, reduce heat and poach fish in barely simmering liquid for 8-10 minutes or until fish flakes easily. Do not overcook.

Remove mahi mahi and reserve one cup of fish stock for sauce.

For Egg Sauce, in a saucepan, over medium heat, melt butter. Stir in flour to make a roux and heat several minutes. Gradually add warm fish stock and cook until thickened. Mix cream and egg yolks. Gradually stir into fish sauce. Do not boil. Fold in eggs and parsley. Heat through.

Pour Egg Sauce onto 6 individual plates and top with mahi mahi. Serve immediately. *Yield: 6 servings.*

4 POUNDS FRESH MUSSELS IN
 THE SHELL
½ CUP WATER
½ CUP DRY WHITE WINE
¼ CUP EXTRA VIRGIN OLIVE OIL
1½ CUPS CHOPPED ONION
1 TABLESPOON MINCED GARLIC
1 GREEN PEPPER, DICED
28 OUNCES ITALIAN-STYLE
 TOMATOES, QUARTERED
½ TEASPOON MINCED
 FRESH BASIL
½ TEASPOON MINCED
 FRESH OREGANO
⅛ TEASPOON SUGAR
⅛ TEASPOON SALT
⅛ TEASPOON FRESHLY
 GROUND PEPPER
½ POUND FRESH
 MUSHROOMS, SLICED
3 TABLESPOONS MINCED
 ITALIAN PARSLEY

MUSSELS WITH MARINARA SAUCE

Scrub mussels under running water. Remove stringy beard from the shells with a knife. Place mussels, water and wine in a large saucepan. Set aside.

In a large skillet heat oil until hot. Add onion and garlic. Cook and stir until golden brown. Stir in green pepper, tomatoes and juices, basil, oregano, sugar, salt, pepper, mushrooms and parsley. Simmer, stirring frequently, for 15 minutes.

Bring the pan of mussels to a boil. Cover tightly and steam just until mussels open slightly, about 3-4 minutes. Do not overcook.

Strain mussels, reserving ½ cup of liquid. Stir reserved liquid into the simmering tomato sauce and adjust seasonings. Add mussels to sauce and serve immediately. *Yield: 4 servings.*

2	FRESH JALAPEÑO PEPPERS
2	GREEN BELL PEPPERS
¾	CUP CHOPPED ONION
½	CUP CHOPPED PARSLEY
¼	CUP PLUS 1 TABLESPOON EXTRA VIRGIN OLIVE OIL
1	CLOVE GARLIC, MINCED
2	TABLESPOONS FRESHLY SQUEEZED LEMON JUICE
	SALT AND FRESHLY GROUND PEPPER
6	PIKE FILLETS
	PARSLEY AS GARNISH

PIKE WITH GREEN SALSA

Preheat broiler. Blacken skins of jalepeño and bell peppers under broiler. Remove from broiler and cover with plastic wrap. After 10 minutes, with hands protected, remove pepper skins under running water. Pat peppers dry, remove seeds and stems and cut into chunks. *Reduce oven to 350° F.*

In a food processor chop peppers, onion and parsley.

In a saucepan heat ¼ cup oil and sauté garlic until soft. Add the pepper mixture and 1 tablespoon of the lemon juice and simmer for 5 minutes. Season salsa with salt and pepper to taste.

Coat bottom of a baking pan with remaining tablespoon oil. Season pike fillets with salt and pepper. Place fish in pan and sprinkle with remaining lemon juice. Bake uncovered until firm but not flaky, about 15-20 minutes.

Transfer fillets to serving platter. Stir pan juices into the salsa and spoon mixture over fish. Garnish with chopped parsley and serve immediately. *Yield: 6 servings.*

1	4-POUND SALMON, BONED WITH HEAD AND TAIL INTACT
	SALT AND FRESHLY GROUND PEPPER
⅓	CUP MINCED PARSLEY
¼	CUP MINCED FRESH DILL
6	SHALLOTS, FINELY CHOPPED
1	LEMON, THINLY SLICED
2	LIMES, THINLY SLICED
1¼	CUPS CLAM JUICE
⅓	CUP DRY WHITE WINE
1	GARLIC CLOVE, MINCED
2	TEASPOONS CHOPPED FRESH THYME
2	CUCUMBERS, SLICED, AS GARNISH
1	PIMENTO, THINLY SLICED, AS GARNISH
	FRESH PARSLEY SPRIGS AS GARNISH
	CAPER SAUCE
1	EGG YOLK
1	TABLESPOON FRESHLY SQUEEZED LEMON JUICE
2	TEASPOONS DIJON MUSTARD
1	TEASPOON MINCED PARSLEY
1	TEASPOON FINELY CHOPPED CHIVES
2	TEASPOONS CHOPPED FRESH DILL
½	TEASPOON SALT
4	TEASPOONS CAPERS, RINSED AND DRAINED
	WHITE PEPPER TO TASTE
⅔	CUP VEGETABLE OIL
1	CUCUMBER, PEELED, SEEDED, FINELY CHOPPED
½	CUP WHIPPING CREAM

POACHED SALMON GOOD WITH CAPER SAUCE

Preheat oven to 450° F. Rinse fish under cold water and pat dry. Season with salt and pepper.

Line a large roasting pan with heavy-duty foil. Place ½ of the parsley, dill, shallots and lemon and lime slices in the cavity of the fish. Place fish in pan.

Combine clam juice, wine, garlic and thyme. Pour over fish.

Cover fish with remaining parsley, dill, shallots and lemon and lime slices.

Place pan with fish over medium heat and bring liquids to a boil. Cover fish loosely with foil. Transfer pan to oven and bake for 40-45 minutes or until fish feels firm to the touch. Remove fish from oven and place on serving platter to cool. Remove skin from top side of fish.

For sauce, in a food processor combine egg yolk, lemon juice, mustard, parsley, chives, dill, salt, 2 teaspoons of the capers and pepper. Process for 15 seconds. With motor running gradually add oil. Transfer mixture to a bowl. Stir in cucumber. Whip cream until stiff. Carefully fold whipped cream into cucumber mixture. Fold in remaining 2 teaspoons of capers.

Spread a thin layer of Caper Sauce over fish. Garnish with cucumber, pimento and parsley. Serve with remaining sauce. *Yield: 8 servings.*

4	SALMON FILLETS
2	TABLESPOONS FRESHLY
	SQUEEZED LIME JUICE
3	TEASPOONS BUTTER, MELTED
	SALT AND FRESHLY
	GROUND PEPPER
	CHOPPED CHIVES AS GARNISH
	LIME WEDGES AS GARNISH
	JALAPEÑO LIME SAUCE
3	TEASPOONS BUTTER
4	JALAPEÑO PEPPERS, SEEDED
	AND CHOPPED
⅔	CUP SOUR CREAM
1½	TEASPOONS FRESHLY SQUEEZED
	LIME JUICE
	SALT AND WHITE PEPPER

SALMON WITH JALAPEÑO LIME SAUCE

Butter a shallow baking dish. Place salmon in dish with skin side down.

Mix lime juice and butter. Brush mixture over salmon. Sprinkle with salt and pepper. Let stand 20 minutes. *Preheat oven to 500° F.*

For Jalapeño Lime Sauce, melt butter in saucepan over medium heat. Add peppers and cook until tender. Add sour cream and stir until thoroughly heated. Do not boil. Stir in lime juice, salt and pepper. Keep warm.

Bake fish until almost opaque, approximately 12 minutes.

Serve with Jalapeño Lime Sauce garnished with chives and lime wedges. *Yield: 4 servings.*

½	CUP FRESHLY SQUEEZED
	ORANGE JUICE
½	CUP DRY WHITE WINE
12	TABLESPOONS UNSALTED
	BUTTER
2	TABLESPOONS WHIPPING CREAM
1	TEASPOON ORANGE ZEST
	SALT TO TASTE
1½	POUNDS SALMON, CUT IN
	¼″ THICK SLICES
	SALT AND FRESHLY
	GROUND PEPPER
	WATERCRESS SPRIGS
	AS GARNISH

SALMON WITH ORANGE BUTTER

Preheat oven to 400 ° F. In a saucepan bring orange juice and wine to a boil and reduce by half. Remove from heat and gradually whisk in butter. Stir in cream, zest and salt to taste.

Place salmon in buttered baking dish, add salt and pepper to taste and bake for 3 minutes or until opaque. Top with orange butter and garnish with watercress. *Yield: 4 servings.*

½ CUP UNSALTED BUTTER
2 TEASPOONS CHOPPED
    FRESH THYME
3 GREEN ONIONS, THINLY SLICED
1 CLOVE GARLIC, MINCED
½ POUND MUSHROOMS, SLICED
½ SWEET RED PEPPER, JULIENNED
¼ CUP DICED GREEN BELL PEPPER
1¼ POUNDS FRESH
    SCALLOPS, RINSED
2 TABLESPOONS FRESHLY
    SQUEEZED LEMON JUICE
¼ CUP DRY WHITE WINE
2 CUPS HOT COOKED RICE
  AVOCADO BUTTER
½ MEDIUM VERY RIPE
    AVOCADO, PEELED,
    PITTED AND CHOPPED
½ CUP BUTTER, AT ROOM
    TEMPERATURE
  SALT AND FRESHLY
    GROUND PEPPER

SHORE SCALLOPS WITH AVOCADO BUTTER

For Avocado Butter combine all ingredients, mix well and set aside.

In a large saucepan melt ¼ cup of the butter. Add thyme, green onions and garlic. Cook until onions are transparent. Add mushrooms and both peppers and sauté until peppers are crisp-tender. Remove from heat and set aside.

In a bowl combine scallops and lemon juice. Set aside.

In a saucepan melt remaining butter. Add scallops and cook until transparent, about 3 minutes. Add the reserved vegetables. Stir in wine and cook uncovered for several minutes until wine reduces.

Serve scallops, vegetables and sauce over hot rice. Top with a dollop of Avocado Butter. *Yield: 4 servings.*

1 CUP EXTRA VIRGIN OLIVE OIL
½ CUP RED WINE VINEGAR
1 TEASPOON LEMON
    PEPPER SEASONING
2 TABLESPOONS CHOPPED
    FRESH BASIL
2 CLOVES GARLIC, MINCED
½ CUP DRY WHITE WINE
8 SOFT SHELL CRABS
½ POUND LINGUINE, COOKED
    AL DENTE
  FRESHLY GRATED
    PARMESAN CHEESE

GRILLED SOFT SHELL CRAB IN BASIL MARINADE

For marinade, combine oil, vinegar, lemon pepper, basil, garlic and wine in a large bowl. Let stand at room temperature for 1 hour.

Add crabs and refrigerate at least 4 hours. Stir occasionally. *Prepare charcoal grill.*

Remove crabs from marinade. Transfer marinade to small saucepan and heat through.

Grill crabs 2 minutes each side, basting with marinade, just until red.

Serve crab and basil marinade over pasta sprinkled with Parmesan cheese. *Yield: 4 servings.*

12	OUNCES SWORDFISH
1	TABLESPOON PLUS 1 TEASPOON PEANUT OIL
1	CUP BROCCOLI FLORETS
1	STALK CELERY, THINLY SLICED
1	GREEN ONION, THINLY SLICED
¾	CUP BEAN SPROUTS
1	TOMATO, CUBED
2	TABLESPOONS SOY SAUCE
½	CUP DRY WHITE WINE
1	CUP COOKED RICE

SWORDFISH STIR-FRY

Slice swordfish into thick julienne strips.

Heat wok and add 1 tablespoon oil. Stir-fry swordfish until no longer pink. Remove from wok and set aside.

Add 1 teaspoon oil and stir-fry broccoli until crisp-tender, about 2 minutes. Add remaining vegetables in order and stir-fry each briefly. Just after adding tomatoes, return swordfish to wok. Add soy sauce and wine, tossing gently to mix all ingredients.

Serve immediately over cooked rice. *Yield: 2 servings.*

1	MEDIUM TOMATO
1	SMALL SCALLION, SLICED
1½	OUNCES FETA CHEESE, FINELY CHOPPED
½	CUP EXTRA VIRGIN OLIVE OIL
1	TABLESPOON FRESHLY SQUEEZED LEMON JUICE
2	TEASPOONS CHOPPED FRESH DILL
	FRESHLY GROUND PEPPER TO TASTE
¼	CUP DIJON MUSTARD
2½	TABLESPOONS RED WINE VINEGAR
1	TEASPOON GARLIC POWDER
1	TEASPOON GROUND OREGANO
½	TEASPOON SALT
4	SWORDFISH STEAKS

GRILLED SWORDFISH WITH TOMATO FETA RELISH

For relish, core tomato and cut in half horizontally. Scoop out pulp and seeds leaving only the outer shell. Cut shell into ¼″ dice and mix with scallion, feta cheese, ¼ cup of the olive oil, lemon juice, dill and pepper.

For glaze, thoroughly mix together mustard, remaining oil, vinegar and seasonings. *Prepare charcoal grill.*

Brush 1 side of each steak with glaze. Grill, glazed side down, to desired doneness. Brush top side with glaze, turn steaks and cook until fish flakes easily with a fork.

Transfer fish to warm plates and top each steak with relish. Serve immediately. *Yield: 4 servings.*

RAINBOW TROUT WITH DIJON MUSTARD

6	RAINBOW TROUT FILLETS, SKIN REMOVED
	SALT AND FRESHLY GROUND PEPPER
¼	CUP BUTTER, MELTED
1	CUP ALMONDS, CRUSHED
2	TABLESPOONS BUTTER
½	CUP SLICED GREEN ONION
3	TABLESPOONS DIJON MUSTARD
¼	CUP DRY WHITE WINE
1	CUP SOUR CREAM
	CILANTRO AS GARNISH

Preheat oven to 325° F. Season trout with salt and pepper. Dip each fillet in the butter and place in a buttered baking dish. Sprinkle almonds over trout. Bake until fish flakes with fork, about 12-15 minutes.

For the sauce, sauté green onions in butter until they are transparent. Add mustard and wine. Cook, stirring occasionally, for 2-3 minutes. Stir in sour cream and heat through. Do not allow to boil. Pour sauce over fillets.

Serve garnished with cilantro. *Yield: 6 servings.*

CHILLED TROUT FILLETS WITH FENNEL SAUCE

1¼	CUPS CHICKEN BROTH
⅓	CUP SLICED LEEK, WHITE PART ONLY
¼	CUP CELERY LEAVES
6	FRESH FENNEL SPRIGS
4	PEPPERCORNS
4	TROUT FILLETS
	FENNEL SAUCE
⅓	CUP LIGHTLY PACKED FRESH FENNEL SPRIGS
¼	CUP SOUR CREAM
2	TABLESPOONS FINELY CHOPPED LEEK, WHITE PART ONLY
2	TABLESPOONS MAYONNAISE
1	TEASPOON DIJON MUSTARD
1	TEASPOON FRESHLY SQUEEZED LEMON JUICE

In a skillet combine broth, leek, celery, fennel and peppercorns. Bring to a boil. Reduce heat, cover and simmer 10 minutes.

Add trout to broth. Return to a boil. Reduce heat, cover and simmer 4-5 minutes or until fish flakes easily with a fork.

Remove fish from skillet cover and chill.

In a food processor combine sauce ingredients. Process until well blended. Place in a bowl, cover and chill.

Serve chilled trout fillets with Fennel Sauce. *Yield: 2 servings.*

¼ CUP EXTRA VIRGIN OLIVE OIL
   JUICE OF 1 LEMON
2 TABLESPOONS FRESH GINGER
   ROOT, PEELED AND MINCED
6 TUNA STEAKS
6 TABLESPOONS BUTTER, AT
   ROOM TEMPERATURE
¼ CUP WASABI
   SALT AND FRESHLY
   GROUND PEPPER

GRILLED TUNA WITH WASABI BUTTER

Prepare charcoal grill. In a small bowl combine oil, lemon juice and ginger. Pour over fish and let stand 20-30 minutes, turning once.

Mix butter and wasabi to form a thick paste. Set aside.

Season steaks lightly with salt and pepper. Grill tuna 8-10 minutes or until opaque in center, turning occasionally, basting often with marinade.

Serve warm with wasabi butter. *Yield: 6 servings.*

8 TUNA STEAKS
⅓ CUP SOY SAUCE
2 TEASPOONS GRATED LIME PEEL
¼ CUP FRESHLY SQUEEZED
   LIME JUICE
2 CLOVES GARLIC, MINCED
1 TABLESPOON DIJON MUSTARD
¼ CUP PEANUT OIL
¼ CUP FINELY CHOPPED SCALLION
½ TEASPOON FRESHLY GROUND
   BLACK PEPPER
1 SCALLION, JULIENNED,
   AS GARNISH
8 STRIPS LIME PEEL AS GARNISH

TUNA STEAKS IN LIME-SOY MARINADE

Arrange fish in a glass baking dish.

In a small bowl combine remaining ingredients, except garnishes, and mix well. Pour over fish. Cover dish and chill at least 3 hours. *Preheat broiler.*

Place fish on broiler pan and broil 3-4 minutes on each side, until flaky.

Remove fish to a platter and pour juices from the broiling pan over the fish. Garnish with scallion and lime peel. *Yield: 8 servings.*

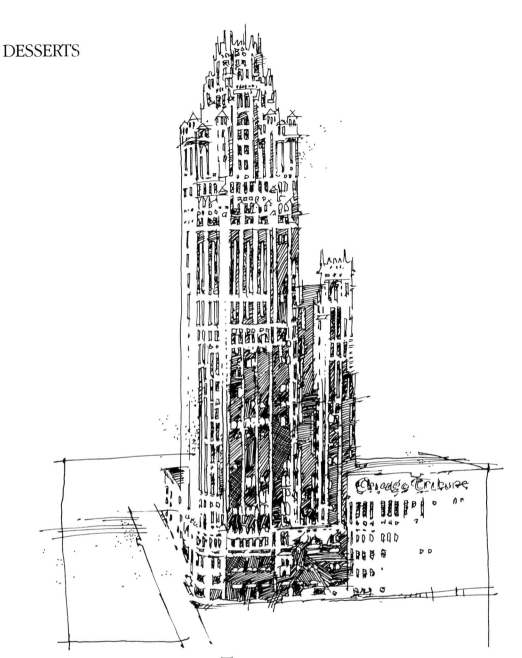

THE TRIBUNE TOWER, home the Chicago *Tribune* newspaper, was built in 1925. Its Gothic Revival style is the result of an international design competition held by Robert R. McCormick, then the newspaper's publisher. The base of the building is studded with stones from such world-famous buildings as Westminster Abbey, L' Arc de Triomphe, St. Peter's in Rome and the Taj Mahal. The building is topped with flying buttresses similar to those of European Gothic cathedrals.

2 CUPS FLOUR
1 TEASPOON BAKING SODA
½ TEASPOON SALT
1 CUP BUTTER
¾ CUP SUGAR
1 CUP FIRMLY PACKED
BROWN SUGAR
1 TEASPOON VANILLA EXTRACT
2 EGGS
12 OUNCES GOURMET SEMISWEET
CHOCOLATE CHUNKS
½ CUP COARSELY
CHOPPED WALNUTS
4 OUNCES CANDY-COATED
CHOCOLATE PIECES

THE BEST CHOCOLATE CHUNK MONSTER COOKIES...EVER

In a small bowl combine flour, soda and salt. Set aside.

In a large bowl combine butter, sugar, brown sugar and vanilla extract. Beat until creamy. Beat in eggs. Gradually add flour mixture and mix well. Stir in chocolate chunks and nuts and mix well. Chill. *Preheat oven to 375° F.*

Drop by rounded tablespoonsful 2″ apart onto greased cookie sheets. Gently press candy-coated pieces into tops of cookies.

Bake 8 to 10 minutes. Cool on cookie sheet 2 minutes. Remove to rack and cool completely. *Yield: 18 to 20 cookies.*

4 OUNCES BUTTER, MELTED
1 CUP EGG WHITES (FROM
APPROXIMATELY 10
LARGE EGGS)
⅔ CUP FLOUR
½ POUND CONFECTIONER'S
SUGAR
2 TEASPOONS VANILLA EXTRACT

TULIP COOKIES

Combine all ingredients and let batter rest for 1-2 hours. *Preheat oven to 375° F.*

Pour ¼ cup batter on each half of a greased cookie sheet. Tip and rotate sheet until there are 2 cookies 5″-6″ in diameter. Do only 2 cookies at a time, as they burn quickly.

Bake until golden brown, 5-6 minutes. Watch closely.

Immediately remove and mold into tulip shape around a 1-cup glass measure, then press in sides to desired shape. Work quickly, as cookie dough hardens rapidly. Invert and fill with ice cream, hot fudge and nuts. *Yield: 8 servings.*

2	MEDIUM EGGS, SLIGHTLY BEATEN
2	CUPS SUGAR
2	TEASPOONS VANILLA EXTRACT
¼	CUP VEGETABLE OIL
1	CUP BUTTER
1	TEASPOON SALT
1½	TEASPOONS BAKING SODA
3	CUPS FLOUR
1½	TEASPOONS CINNAMON
1	TEASPOON MACE
1	TEASPOON FRESHLY GRATED NUTMEG
3	CUPS GRANNY SMITH OR OTHER TART APPLES, PEELED, SEEDED AND CHOPPED
1	CUP PECANS, CHOPPED
	TOPPING
½	CUP FLOUR
1	TEASPOON CINNAMON
¼	CUP SUGAR
¼	CUP CHOPPED PECANS
3	TABLESPOONS BUTTER, AT ROOM TEMPERATURE

FRESH APPLE CAKE WITH PENUCHE FROSTING

Preheat oven to 375° F. In a large bowl thoroughly mix together eggs and sugar. Add vanilla, oil and butter and mix well.

In a separate bowl sift together salt, baking soda, flour, cinnamon, mace and nutmeg. Add to egg mixture and combine well. Stir in apples and pecans. Mixture will be stiff and heavy.

Pour into greased and floured 12-cup tube pan.

Combine topping ingredients. Crumble on top of batter in tube pan.

Bake for 1 hour. Cool and serve with Penuche Frosting (recipe follows). *Yield: 12 servings.*

½	CUP BUTTER
1	CUP FIRMLY PACKED BROWN SUGAR
¼	CUP WHOLE MILK, HEATED
3¼	CUPS CONFECTIONER'S SUGAR
¼	CUP CHOPPED WALNUTS

PENUCHE FROSTING

Melt butter in saucepan. Add brown sugar. Bring to a boil. Cook 1 minute, stirring constantly or until slightly thickened. Cool 15 minutes.

Add hot milk and beat until smooth. Beat in confectioner's sugar until mixture achieves spreading consistency. Use frosting immediately.

Top with a sprinkle of chopped walnuts.

PASTRY FOR 9″
    SINGLE-CRUST PIE
16   OUNCES PUMPKIN, MASHED
¾   CUP SUGAR
1   TEASPOON PUMPKIN PIE SPICE
3   EGGS
⅔   CUP EVAPORATED MILK
½   CUP MILK
½   CUP SEMISWEET
    CHOCOLATE PIECES
    WHIPPED CREAM AS GARNISH
TOPPING
½   CUP COARSELY
    CHOPPED PECANS
¼   CUP SUGAR
1   TABLESPOON BUTTER

CHOCOLATE PRALINE PUMPKIN PIE

Prepare and roll out pastry. Line a 9″ pie plate with pastry. Flute edge high. Do not prick pastry.

In a large bowl stir together the pumpkin, sugar and pumpkin pie spice. Add eggs and beat lightly. Stir in both milks. Transfer ½ cup of the pumpkin mixture to a small saucepan. Pour remaining pumpkin mixture into prepared pastry. *Preheat oven to 375° F.*

Add chocolate pieces to pumpkin mixture in the saucepan. Cook over low heat, stirring constantly, until melted.

Spoon chocolate mixture over filling in pastry. To marble, use a narrow spatula to gently swirl through mixture.

Cover edge of pie with foil. Bake for 25 minutes. Remove foil and bake 25-30 minutes or until knife inserted near center of pie comes out clean. Remove from oven and cool thoroughly on a wire rack.

While pie is cooling combine topping ingredients in a saucepan. Cook over medium heat, stirring constantly for 6-8 minutes or until sugar melts and turns a rich, brown color. Spread mixture on a buttered baking sheet and separate into small chunks. Let cool. Sprinkle on top of pumpkin pie and serve with a dollop of whipped cream on each slice. *Yield: 8 servings.*

8-10   OUNCES FUDGE COOKIES,
    FINELY GROUND
⅓   CUP SUGAR
4   OUNCES BUTTER, SOFTENED
8   OUNCES CREAM
    CHEESE, SOFTENED
1   CUP CHUNKY PEANUT BUTTER
1   CUP CONFECTIONER'S SUGAR
1   CUP WHIPPING
    CREAM, WHIPPED

CHICAGO PEANUT BUTTER PIE

Preheat oven to 350° F. Combine cookie crumbs, sugar and butter.

Press mixture into a 9″ pie plate and bake for 15 minutes. Cool.

In a food processor combine cream cheese, peanut butter and confectioner's sugar. Process until almost smooth. Gently stir in whipped cream and pour into pie shell. Chill. *Yield: 8 servings.*

CHOCOLATE CHIP WALNUT PIE

2	LARGE EGGS
½	CUP FLOUR
½	CUP SUGAR
½	CUP FIRMLY PACKED BROWN SUGAR
1	CUP UNSALTED BUTTER, MELTED
6	OUNCES SEMISWEET CHOCOLATE CHIPS
1	CUP CHOPPED WALNUTS
1	9″ UNBAKED PIE SHELL OR WALNUT PIE PASTRY (RECIPE FOLLOWS) WHIPPED CREAM OR VANILLA ICE CREAM

Preheat oven to 325° F. Beat eggs in large bowl until foamy. Gradually beat in flour and sugars until well blended. Add butter and beat until smooth. Fold in chocolate chips and nuts. Pour into unbaked pie shell.

Bake about 50 minutes, until toothpick inserted in center comes out clean. Cool completely.

Serve topped with whipped cream or ice cream.
Yield: 6 to 8 servings.

WALNUT PIE PASTRY

5	OUNCES WALNUT PIECES
1½	CUPS FLOUR
½	TEASPOON SALT
½	CUP COLD BUTTER, CUT IN PIECES
1	LARGE EGG YOLK DRY BEANS, TO WEIGHT

In a food processor combine walnuts, flour and salt. Process until finely ground. Add butter and process to fine crumbs, 1-2 minutes. Add egg yolk. Pulse just until dough forms a ball. If dough seems dry, add 1 tablespoon water.

Turn dough onto floured work surface. Knead lightly 1-2 minutes until it forms a smooth ball. Wrap in plastic. Chill at least 30 minutes. Roll out to fit a 9″ pie plate.

Line pie pan with pastry and prick bottom with fork. Chill shell until firm, 20-30 minutes. Cover shell with waxed paper and weight with dry beans. *Preheat oven to 400° F.*

Bake until pastry is set and beginning to brown, 10-15 minutes. Remove beans and paper; bake shell 5-7 minutes longer, until bottom of crust is no longer soft.

Remove from oven. Cool completely. *Yield: One 9″ pie crust.*

BLACKBERRY PLUM PIE

PASTRY FOR 10″
DOUBLE-CRUST PIE
1½ POUNDS FRIAR PLUMS, PITTED
AND CUT INTO 1″ PIECES
¾ CUP SUGAR
⅓ CUP FLOUR
GRATED ZEST OF 1 LEMON
2 TABLESPOONS GIN
PINCH GROUND CLOVES
1 PINT FRESH BLACKBERRIES
3 AMARETTO COOKIES,
FINELY CRUSHED
1 TABLESPOON UNSALTED
BUTTER

Roll half the pastry to fit a 10″ pie plate. Place pastry into pie plate and crimp edges; freeze. Roll other half of pastry into an 11″ circle and cut into ten 1″ lattice strips. Place on baking sheet and refrigerate.

In a bowl toss plums, sugar, flour, lemon zest, gin and cloves. Fold in blackberries. *Preheat oven to 425° F.*

Sprinkle cookie crumbs on bottom of pie shell. Pile fruit on top and dot with butter. Weave lattice strips on top, pressing edges into bottom crust.

Bake 10 minutes. *Reduce heat to 350° F.* Bake an additional 1½ hours or until bubbly. Cool. *Yield: 6 to 8 servings.*

HAZELNUT CHOCOLATE MOUSSE

1 TEASPOON UNFLAVORED
GELATIN
¼ CUP COLD WATER
3 OUNCES SEMISWEET
CHOCOLATE
1 OUNCE UNSWEETENED
CHOCOLATE
6½ OUNCES HAZELNUT SPREAD
¼ CUP COFFEE-FLAVORED
LIQUEUR
5 EGGS, SEPARATED
2 CUPS WHIPPING CREAM
CHOCOLATE SHAVINGS
AS GARNISH

In a small bowl mix gelatin with cold water and let soften 10 minutes. When softened, set bowl over hot water until ready to use.

Melt both chocolates, over low heat, in a double boiler. Add hazelnut spread and stir until thoroughly blended. Add liqueur and stir.

In a medium bowl combine egg yolks with chocolate mixture and blend well. Stir dissolved gelatin into chocolate mixture and chill 5 minutes.

Whip egg whites until stiff. Thoroughly mix half of egg whites into chocolate. Gently fold remaining egg whites into chocolate.

Whip the cream and fold into chocolate. Turn out into a large serving bowl or individual bowls and chill several hours. Garnish with chocolate shavings. *Yield: 6 to 8 servings.*

2	CUPS APPLE JUICE
1	CUP WATER
2	CUPS SUGAR
4	CUPS CRANBERRIES
2	TABLESPOONS FRESHLY SQUEEZED LEMON JUICE
¼	TEASPOON SALT
1	CUP COLD MILK
2	EGG WHITES, STIFFLY BEATEN
8	MINT LEAVES AS GARNISH

CRANBERRY SORBET

In a large saucepan combine apple juice, water and sugar. Bring to a boil and cook for 5 minutes until sugar dissolves. Add cranberries, lemon juice and salt. Simmer until the cranberries have popped. Cook an additional 2 minutes. Strain the mixture. Stir in milk.

Place mixture in a shallow 9″ x 13″ pan and freeze for 2-3 hours or until partially set. Spoon mixture into large bowl and beat until smooth. Fold in egg whites. Return to freezer for 2 hours. When partially frozen, beat again. Spoon into individual serving dishes and serve when nearly frozen solid. Garnish with mint leaves. *Yield: 8 servings.*

¼	CUP UNSALTED BUTTER
¼	CUP FLOUR
1	TEASPOON GROUND GINGER
1	CUP WARM MILK
4	EGGS, SEPARATED, AT ROOM TEMPARATURE
⅓	CUP SUGAR
1	TEASPOON VANILLA EXTRACT
3	TABLESPOONS FINELY CHOPPED CANDIED GINGER
¼	TEASPOON CREAM OF TARTAR CANDIED GINGER DIPPED IN MELTED, SEMISWEET CHOCOLATE AS GARNISH
	CHOCOLATE SAUCE
2	TABLESPOONS UNSALTED BUTTER
½	CUP SUGAR
½	CUP DUTCH COCOA
2	CUPS WHIPPING CREAM

GINGER SOUFFLÉ WITH CHOCOLATE SAUCE

In a saucepan melt butter. Whisk in flour and ginger. Add warm milk and whisk over medium heat until smooth. Set aside to cool.

In a bowl beat egg yolks until thick and light. Whisk in sugar and vanilla. Whisk into white sauce mixture. Stir in candied ginger.

For sauce, in a pan melt butter over medium heat. Add sugar and whisk together. Add cocoa and whisk. Add cream and whisk. Reduce heat to simmer and cook 5 minutes. Remove from heat. Cool. Cover surface of sauce with plastic wrap. Sauce may be chilled. Bring to room temperature for serving. *Preheat oven to 400° F.*

In another bowl beat egg whites and cream of tartar until egg whites stand in stiff peaks. Fold egg whites into yolk mixture.

Pour into 8 unbuttered individual soufflé dishes and set in roasting pan. Add enough warm water to come halfway up sides of soufflé dishes. Bake 10-12 minutes or until puffed and golden but not dry. Serve immediately with chocolate-dipped candied ginger and Chocolate Sauce. *Yield: 8 servings.*

2¼ CUPS FLOUR
½ CUP PLUS 2
    TABLESPOONS SUGAR
1½ TEASPOONS SALT
8 OUNCES UNSALTED BUTTER,
    CHILLED AND CUT INTO
    SMALL PIECES
4½ TABLESPOONS ICE WATER
2 PINTS FRESH BLACKBERRIES
    OR RASPBERRIES
2 TABLESPOONS UNSALTED
    BUTTER, MELTED

BLACKBERRY ROLL

In a food processor combine flour, 2 tablespoons of the sugar, salt and 6 ounces of the chilled butter. Pulse until mixture resembles coarse meal. Add 4½ tablespoons ice water and process until mixture is just beginning to form a ball. Remove from processor and wrap in plastic wrap. Refrigerate.

In a medium bowl combine 1½ pints of the blackberries and ¼ cup of the sugar. Set aside.

On a floured surface roll out the chilled dough into a 9″ x 15″ rectangle, ¼″ thick. *Preheat oven to 450° F.*

Brush dough with melted butter and top with berry mixture. Dot with remaining chilled butter and roll up as in a jelly roll.

Place seam-side-down in a buttered 9″ x 13″ baking dish. Cut several diagonal slits in top of roll. Sprinkle with remaining sugar and distribute remaining blackberries around roll. Bake 10 minutes. Carefully pour ½ cup hot water around the base of the roll. *Lower oven temperature to 350° F* and bake 40 to 45 minutes. Remove from oven, slice and spoon juices on top. *Yield: 6 to 8 servings.*

¼ POUND BUTTER
1 CUP FLOUR
½ CUP SOUR CREAM
8 OUNCES APRICOT JAM
⅔ CUP COCONUT, SHREDDED
½ CUP CHOPPED PISTACHIO NUTS,
    PECANS OR ALMONDS

PERSIAN SLICES

In a bowl combine butter, flour and sour cream. Mix well. Form into a ball and wrap in plastic wrap. Chill 6 hours. *Preheat oven to 350° F.*

On a floured surface roll out dough into a rectangle ⅛″ to ¼″ thick.

Spread dough with apricot jam and sprinkle with coconut and nuts.

Roll up as in a jelly roll. Bake for 25 minutes or until lightly browned. Remove to wire rack and cool. Slice into ⅝″ slices. *Yield: 6 to 8 servings.*

PECAN CHOCOLATE BUTTERSCOTCH BARS

2	CUPS FLOUR
1½	CUPS FIRMLY PACKED BROWN SUGAR
½	CUP BUTTER, SOFTENED
1	CUP PECAN HALVES
⅔	CUP BUTTER
½	CUP BUTTERSCOTCH PIECES
½	CUP SEMISWEET CHOCOLATE PIECES

Preheat oven to 350° F. With an electric mixer beat flour, 1 cup of the brown sugar and ½ cup butter, scraping sides of bowl often, until creamed.

Press into an ungreased 9″ x 13″ pan. Sprinkle with pecan halves.

In a medium saucepan, over medium heat, melt ⅔ cup butter. Add remaining brown sugar, stirring constantly until mixture boils, about 4-5 minutes. Boil 1 minute longer, stirring constantly. Pour mixture evenly over mixture in pan.

Bake for 18-20 minutes or until mixture is bubbly. Remove from oven and immediately sprinkle butterscotch and chocolate pieces evenly over top. Allow to melt slightly, then swirl pieces as they melt for a marbled effect. Cool completely and cut into bars. *Yield: 36 bars.*

RASPBERRY WALNUT SNOW BARS

1¼	CUPS PLUS 2 TABLESPOONS SIFTED FLOUR
½	CUP SUGAR
½	CUP BUTTER
⅓	CUP RASPBERRY JAM
2	EGGS
½	CUP FIRMLY PACKED BROWN SUGAR
1	TEASPOON VANILLA EXTRACT PINCH OF SALT
⅛	TEASPOON BAKING SODA
1	CUP CHOPPED WALNUTS

Preheat oven to 350° F. Combine 1¼ cups of the flour and sugar. Cut in butter until mixture resembles fine meal and press into a lightly greased 9″ square baking pan. Bake for 20 minutes until edges turn light brown.

Remove from oven and cover the crust with raspberry jam.

Beat eggs with brown sugar and vanilla until well blended. Stir in 2 tablespoons flour, salt and baking soda. Add walnuts and mix. Spoon over jam and spread lightly to corners of pan. Return pan to oven and bake an additional 20-25 minutes until topping is set. Cool in pan and cut into squares. *Yield: 18 squares.*

DOUGH

½	CUP BUTTER
¼	CUP SUGAR
1	EGG
½	TEASPOON VANILLA EXTRACT
1¼	CUPS SIFTED FLOUR
⅛	TEASPOON SALT

FILLING

2	EGGS, BEATEN
1½	CUPS FIRMLY PACKED BROWN SUGAR
1	CUP CHOPPED PECANS
½	CUP GRATED COCONUT
2	TABLESPOONS FLOUR
½	TEASPOON BAKING POWDER
½	TEASPOON SALT
1	TEASPOON VANILLA EXTRACT

ICING

1½	CUPS CONFECTIONER'S SUGAR
	FRESHLY SQUEEZED LEMON JUICE

LEMON COCONUTTY SQUARES

Preheat oven to 350° F. For dough, cream butter and sugar until well blended. Beat in egg, vanilla, flour and salt. Mix well and spread dough evenly into a 9″ x 13″ pan. Bake for 15 minutes. Cool.

For filling, combine all ingredients and spread over cooled crust. Bake 15 minutes. Cool.

For icing, thin confectioner's sugar with fresh lemon juice and spread on top of cooled filling. *Yield: 24 squares.*

3	NAVEL ORANGES, PEELED AND CUT INTO ⅓″ SLICES
¼	CUP PITTED DATES, MINCED
¼	CUP DARK RUM
3	TABLESPOONS PINE NUTS, LIGHTLY TOASTED

MACERATED ORANGES AND DATES WITH PINE NUTS

Arrange oranges in a serving dish. Top with dates and sprinkle mixture with rum.

Let the mixture macerate, covered and chilled, for at least 1 hour. Serve sprinkled with pine nuts. *Yield: 4 servings.*

FRESH BERRIES WITH WHIPPED ZABAGLIONE SAUCE

3	EGGS
¾	CUP SUGAR
½	CUP DRY WHITE WINE
1	CUP WHIPPING
	CREAM, WHIPPED
1	PINT FRESH BLUEBERRIES
1	PINT FRESH RASPBERRIES

In top of double boiler whisk eggs, sugar and wine until well blended and light in color. Place pan over simmering water in bottom of double boiler and whisk until sauce thickens. Remove from heat and cool completely.

Stir in whipped cream and pour over chilled berries.
Yield: 4 servings.

PERSIMMON PUDDING AND SAUCE

3	MEDIUM EGGS
1¼	CUPS SUGAR
4	OUNCES BUTTER, MELTED
2	CUPS BUTTERMILK
2	CUPS FLOUR
1	TEASPOON BAKING SODA
½	TEASPOON BAKING POWDER
1	TEASPOON SALT
2	TEASPOONS CINNAMON
½	TEASPOON GROUND GINGER
½	TEASPOON FRESHLY GROUND NUTMEG
	DASH GROUND CLOVES
	DASH MACE
2	CUPS PERSIMMON PULP
1	TEASPOON VANILLA EXTRACT
1	CUP CHOPPED WALNUTS OR RAISINS, OPTIONAL

PERSIMMON SAUCE

1	CUP SUGAR
2	TABLESPOONS FLOUR
1	CUP BOILING WATER
1	TEASPOON BUTTER
1	TEASPOON VANILLA EXTRACT

Preheat oven to 325° F. Beat together eggs and sugar. Stir in butter and buttermilk.

Sift together dry ingredients and add them to the the egg mixture.

Add persimmon pulp; mix well. Add vanilla and nuts or raisins.

Pour into 2 greased 8″ square baking pans. Bake 1¼ hours.

For sauce, in a saucepan mix together sugar and flour. Add water, bring to a boil and boil for 1 minute. Remove from heat, add butter and vanilla. Stir to combine. Serve warm over Persimmon Pudding. *Yield: 12 servings.*

NOTE: To make persimmon pulp put overripe persimmon through a food mill, separating seeds from pulp.

5	RIPE PEARS, PEELED, AND CORED
½	CUP FRESHLY SQUEEZED LEMON JUICE
¾	CUP SUGAR
1	CUP WATER
2	TABLESPOONS PEAR WILLIAM LIQUEUR

PEAR ICE

Combine pears and lemon juice in food processor or blender. Process until smooth. Add sugar, water and liqueur. Process well.

Pour mixture into nonaluminum metal bowl, cover, place in freezer. Remove from freezer every few hours to beat with electric mixer.

After last beating, spoon into individual serving bowls while pear ice is light and fluffy. *Yield: 4 to 6 servings.*

½	CUP SUGAR
1	CUP WATER
6	CUPS RIESLING OR CHENIN BLANC WINE
2	TABLESPOONS FRESHLY SQUEEZED LEMON JUICE
10	MINT LEAVES AS GARNISH
10	CANDIED VIOLETS AS GARNISH

RIESLING ICE

Cook sugar and water in medium saucepan over low heat, swirling pan occassionally, until sugar dissolves.

Increase heat to medium-high and boil 5 minutes.

Blend in wine and lemon juice. Cool. Transfer to a metal bowl or pan and freeze. Use a fork or small whisk every few hours to stir and break up ice crystals during freezing.

Scoop ice into individual sherbet dishes. Garnish with mint leaves and candied violets. *Yield: 10 servings.*

1	PINT FRESH BLACKBERRIES
¾	CUP SUGAR
1	TEASPOON FRESHLY SQUEEZED LEMON JUICE

BLACKBERRY ICE

In small nonaluminum pan bring berries and sugar to a boil over medium heat. Simmer 5 minutes and add lemon juice. Strain all seeds.

Add ¾ cup water to berry mixture and pour into nonaluminum dish. Place in freezer and stir every 20-30 minutes until frozen. *Yield: 6 servings.*

FRESH STUFFED PEACHES

5	LARGE FRESH PEACHES, HALVED, PITTED
10	AMARETTO COOKIES, CRUSHED
	UNSALTED BUTTER, SOFTENED
¼	CUP FIRMLY PACKED BROWN SUGAR
¼	CUP AMARETTO LIQUEUR
	WHIPPED CREAM AS GARNISH

Preheat oven to 375° F. Place peaches, cut side up, in buttered 9" x 13" baking dish. Fill enlarged peach centers with crushed cookie crumbs. Place small pat of butter over each. Sprinkle with sugar and bake for 15 minutes. Sprinkle tops with liqueur and bake an additional 15 minutes.

Serve warm or chilled with whipped cream. *Yield: 5 servings.*

CHAMPAGNE POACHED PEARS

4	CUPS CHAMPAGNE
¼	CUP FRAMBOISE LIQUEUR
1⅓	CUPS SUGAR
1	VANILLA BEAN
12	SMALL, FIRM, RIPE PEARS, PEELED, HALVED AND PITTED
	CRÈME FRAÎCHE OR WHIPPED CREAM
½	TEASPOON VANILLA EXTRACT
	CONFECTIONER'S SUGAR TO TASTE

In a large saucepan combine champagne, framboise, sugar and vanilla bean. Bring to a boil. Stir occasionally and cook for 10 minutes.

Reduce heat and add pears. Poach 5 to 10 minutes, until pears are tender but not soft, turning pears in liquid once or twice.

Remove saucepan from heat. Let pears steep in liquid at least one hour to absorb flavors.

Combine crème fraîche, vanilla extract and sugar to taste. Remove pears from liquid and serve with crème fraîche. *Yield: 6 servings.*

3	POUNDS OF MIXED FRUITS (PEACHES, APRICOTS, NECTARINES) PEELED, PITTED AND THINLY SLICED
2	CUPS WATER
2	CUPS SEMI-DRY WHITE WINE
¼	CUP SUGAR
1	2″ PIECE VANILLA BEAN, SPLIT LENGTHWISE
¼	TEASPOON FRESHLY GRATED NUTMEG
	YOGURT AS GARNISH

FRUIT SOUP

In a saucepan, combine all ingredients except yogurt. Bring to a simmer over medium heat. Reduce heat to low. Simmer until fruit is tender, 12 to 15 minutes.

Pour into a bowl. Cover. Chill 4 hours.

Serve with a large dollop of yogurt. *Yield: 6 to 8 servings.*

2	CUPS PITTED SOUR CHERRIES
5½	CUPS WATER
½	CUP SUGAR
½	LEMON, THINLY SLICED
1	STICK CINNAMON
3	TABLESPOONS CORNSTARCH
½	TEASPOON SALT
½	TEASPOON ALMOND EXTRACT
½	TEASPOON RED FOOD COLORING
	SOUR CREAM AS GARNISH

ICED CHERRY SOUP

In a large saucepan, slightly mash cherries. Add 5 cups of the water, sugar, lemon slices and cinnamon. Cover. Cook over low heat for 30 minutes.

Dissolve cornstarch in remaining ½ cup water. Add to cherry mixture with salt, almond extract and coloring. Cook until soup clears and begins to thicken. Chill.

Serve garnished with sour cream. *Yield: 6 servings.*

1	LARGE NAVEL ORANGE
2¼	POUNDS VERY RIPE MANGOES, PEELED AND PITTED
1½	CUPS BUTTERMILK
1½	CUPS FRESHLY SQUEEZED ORANGE JUICE
2	TEASPOONS HONEY
1	TABLESPOON FRESHLY SQUEEZED LEMON JUICE
8	SMALL, FRESH MINT LEAVES AS GARNISH

ORANGE MANGO SOUP

Remove the rind from the orange with a citrus zester or grater and reserve. Remove all the peel and white pith. Cut the orange horizontally into eight slices and refrigerate.

In a food processor purée mangoes with the orange rind. Strain into a 1½-quart bowl.

Combine reserved orange slices, mango purée, buttermilk, orange juice, honey and lemon juice. Chill. Serve garnished with mint leaves. *Yield: 4 servings.*

1	POUND FRESH, RIPE STRAWBERRIES
1	PINT STRONG CHICKEN BROTH
1	SMALL CLOVE GARLIC, PEELED
1	PINT WHIPPING CREAM
	SALT AND FRESHLY GROUND PEPPER TO TASTE
6	SRAWBERRIES, SLICED AS GARNISH

ICED STRAWBERRY SOUP

In a food processor purée strawberries, broth and garlic.

Strain to remove strawberry seeds. Stir in cream. Salt and pepper to taste.

Serve well chilled with a sliced strawberry garnish. *Yield: 4 to 6 servings.*

SAUCES & DRESSINGS

CHICAGO'S WATER TOWER, perhaps the city's best-known and loved landmark, stands proudly on the corner of Chicago and Michigan Avenues. Built from 1867 to 1869, this pseudo-Gothic structure was designed to conceal a standpipe for the water pumping station across the street. This pumping station is still in operation; it pumps three billion gallons of water—40% of Chicago's supply—every day. The Water Tower is noteworthy not only for its architecture but also because it was one of the few buildings to survive the Great Chicago Fire of 1871.

1   CUP APRICOT PRESERVES
1-2 TABLESPOONS WATER
1   TABLESPOON KIRSCH

APRICOT SAUCE

In a small saucepan, combine preserves and water. Cook on low heat until melted. Strain to remove fruit. Cool slightly. Add kirsch and mix well. *Yield: 1 cup.*

NOTE: Use on ice cream or pound cake or as a glaze on fruit tarts.

2   EGG YOLKS
4   TABLESPOONS SUGAR
1   TEASPOON FLOUR
2   TEASPOONS VANILLA EXTRACT
1   CUP MILK

CRÈME ANGLAISE

In a small bowl whisk egg yolks with sugar until the mixture is bright yellow. Add the flour and vanilla and whisk again.

In a medium saucepan bring the milk to a boil.

While whisking, pour the boiling milk over the yolk-sugar mixture, then return to pan. While stirring constantly bring the mixture to a boil. Immediately remove pan from heat, whisking to cool. Pour through a fine sieve for the best texture. *Yield: 1 1/2 cups.*

NOTE: For a chocolate sauce, add 2 ounces chopped bittersweet chocolate to the hot sauce and stir until melted. For a mocha sauce, add 2-3 teaspoons powdered instant espresso coffee. For an orange sauce, add 2 tablespoons orange-flavored liqueur.

2½ CUPS GOLDEN RAISINS
2   CUPS FRESHLY SQUEEZED
       ORANGE JUICE
1   CUP WATER
¼   CUP FRESHLY SQUEEZED
       LEMON JUICE
1   CUP SUGAR
3   CUPS CRANBERRIES
1   TABLESPOON GRATED
       ORANGE RIND

RAISINBERRY SAUCE

In a saucepan combine raisins, orange juice, water, lemon juice and sugar. Bring to a boil, stirring until sugar dissolves. Reduce heat and simmer 10 minutes, stirring occasionally.

Add cranberries and orange rind and boil 5 minutes or until berries start to pop. Cool. *Yield: 4 1/2 cups.*

NOTE: Serve with ham, pork or game.

1	CUP PLUS 2 TABLESPOONS FRUIT JUICE
¼	CUP SUGAR, OPTIONAL
1	TABLESPOON FRESHLY SQUEEZED LEMON JUICE
1	PINCH CREAM OF TARTAR
1	TEASPOON CORNSTARCH

FABULOUS FRUIT SAUCE

In a saucepan mix 1 cup of the fruit juice, sugar and lemon juice. Heat to a boil.

Mix cream of tartar and cornstarch with remaining 2 tablespoons fruit juice and add to boiling juice. Cook until clear and slightly thickened. *Yield: 1¼ cups.*

NOTE: Serve hot or cold.

3	OUNCES UNSWEETENED CHOCOLATE
2	TABLESPOONS UNSALTED BUTTER
⅓	CUP BOILING WATER
1	CUP SUGAR
1	TABLESPOON CORN SYRUP

HOT FUDGE SAUCE

In a double boiler, over hot water, add chocolate and heat until melted. Immediately add butter, stirring constantly. Add water, sugar and corn syrup. Heat to a boil over a low direct heat. Do not stir. Cook 5 minutes for regular hot fudge sauce. Cook 8 minutes for a sauce that will harden over ice cream. To keep warm, place in hot water. *Yield: ¾ cup.*

¾	CUP SUGAR
⅓	CUP UNSWEETENED COCOA POWDER
⅔	CUP EVAPORATED MILK
¼	CUP CHUNKY PEANUT BUTTER

MISSISSIPPI MUD SAUCE

In a small saucepan stir together sugar and cocoa powder. Stir in evaporated milk and bring to a boil over medium heat. Remove from heat and stir in peanut butter. *Yield: 1½ cups.*

NOTE: Serve warm over ice cream.

½	CUP UNSALTED BUTTER, AT ROOM TEMPERATURE
½	CUP CONFECTIONER'S SUGAR
½	TEASPOON VANILLA EXTRACT OR FRUIT FLAVORED LIQUEUR

HEAVENLY HARD SAUCE

In a small bowl cream butter. Gradually add sugar and whip. Stir in the flavoring. Chill 1 hour before serving. *Yield: ¾ cup.*

1   BUNCH ARUGULA
½   CUP BUTTER
1   TABLESPOON FRESHLY
        SQUEEZED LEMON JUICE

....

ARUGULA BUTTER

In a food processor combine all ingredients. Process just until mixed. *Yield: ³⁄₄ cup.*

½   CUP UNSALTED
        BUTTER, SOFTENED
¼   CUP CHOPPED FRESH PARSLEY
1   TABLESPOON GREEN
        PEPPERCORNS, DRAINED
1   TEASPOON FRESHLY SQUEEZED
        LEMON JUICE
½   TEASPOON DIJON MUSTARD
     WORCESTERSHIRE SAUCE
        TO TASTE

....

GREEN PEPPERCORN BUTTER

In a food processor combine all ingredients and blend well. Add salt if desired. Refrigerate. *Yield: ¹⁄₂ cup*

NOTE: Serve with grilled meats.

2   MEDIUM AVOCADOS, PEELED,
        SEEDED AND CUBED
¼   CUP HALF-AND-HALF
3   TABLESPOONS DRY WHITE WINE
        OR DRY VERMOUTH
1   TABLESPOON FRESHLY
        SQUEEZED LEMON JUICE
1   TABLESPOON MINCED
        FRESH PARSLEY
1   TABLESPOON MINCED
        FRESH CHIVES
1   TEASPOON GARLIC SALT
2   TEASPOONS FRESH THYME
½   TEASPOON WHITE PEPPER

....

AVOCADO BUTTER

Combine all ingredients in a food processor. Process until smooth. Chill until ready to serve. *Yield: 1¹⁄₂ cups.*

NOTE: Use with omelets, grilled meat or fish.

½ CUP BUTTER

GRATED RIND AND JUICE OF
½ LEMON

1 TABLESPOON FINELY
CHOPPED SCALLIONS

¼ TEASPOON SEASONED SALT

⅛ TEASPOON FRESHLY
GROUND PEPPER

LEMON BUTTER PATTIES

In a small bowl combine all ingredients. On waxed paper, shape mixture into a 1″ x 7″ roll. Chill. Slice and serve over fish. *Yield: ½ cup.*

NOTE: Can be melted and used as a basting sauce.

2 CUPS PITTED PRUNES

1¾ CUPS APPLE JUICE

4 DRIED FIGS, STEMS REMOVED

1 VANILLA BEAN

PINCH OF FRESHLY GRATED
ORANGE PEEL

PRUNE BUTTER

In a large saucepan combine all ingredients. Bring to a simmer and cook, stirring frequently, for 25-30 minutes. Let the mixture cool slightly. Discard the vanilla bean. Transfer mixture to a food processor and process until smooth. *Yield: 2 cups.*

NOTE: Serve with breakfast breads or muffins.

1 TABLESPOON VEGETABLE OIL

2 TABLESPOONS FRESH GINGER
ROOT, MINCED

1 TEASPOON MINCED
FRESH GARLIC

¼ CUP MINCED GREEN ONION

1 CUP WHIPPING CREAM

¼ TEASPOON CURRY POWDER

2 TABLESPOONS CHUTNEY

⅛ TEASPOON SALT

⅛ TEASPOON CAYENNE PEPPER

2½ TABLESPOONS PLAIN YOGURT

2 TABLESPOONS MINCED PARSLEY

CREAMY CURRY DRESSING WITH CHUTNEY AND GINGER

In a large skillet heat oil. Add ginger root, garlic and onion. Sauté until tender, about 1½ minutes.

Slowly stir in cream. Simmer until liquid reduces enough to lightly coat a spoon. Stir in curry powder and simmer 1 minute. Stir in chutney, salt and cayenne. Remove from heat and stir in yogurt and parsley. *Yield: 1½ cups.*

NOTE: Makes an excellent dressing for crisp salad greens.

1½ CUPS MAYONNAISE
1½ CUPS PLAIN YOGURT
3 TABLESPOONS TOMATO PASTE
JUICE OF ½ LEMON

LIGHT TOMATO MAYONNAISE

Whisk together all ingredients. *Yield: 3¼ cups.*

NOTE: Serve with fish or salads.

¼ CUP FRESH SPINACH,
FIRMLY PACKED
1 LARGE EGG YOLK
1 TABLESPOON DIJON MUSTARD
½ TEASPOON FRESHLY SQUEEZED
LEMON JUICE
¼ TEASPOON SALT
FRESHLY GROUND PEPPER
1 CUP VEGETABLE OIL

SPINACH DIJON MAYONNAISE

In a food processor combine spinach, egg yolk, mustard, lemon juice, salt, pepper and 3 tablespoons of the oil. Process until slightly thickened.

With the motor running, slowly add remaining oil and process until thickened. *Yield: 1 cup.*

NOTE: Watercress may be substituted for the spinach. Delicious served with crudités, sandwiches, vegetables or fish.

1 CUP MAYONNAISE
1 TABLESPOON FRESH
TARRAGON, MINCED
1 TABLESPOON FRESH
BASIL, MINCED
2 TEASPOONS FRESHLY SQUEEZED
LEMON JUICE
SALT AND WHITE PEPPER
TO TASTE

HERB MAYONNAISE FOR FISH OR POULTRY

In a small bowl combine all ingredients. Blend well and correct seasoning. Set aside 1 hour. *Yield: ¾ cup.*

1 MEDIUM ONION, MINCED
½ CUP VEGETABLE OIL
2 TABLESPOONS CATSUP
2 TABLESPOONS BROWN SUGAR
2 TEASPOONS WORCESTERSHIRE
SAUCE
1½ TEASPOONS DRY MUSTARD

SEAFOOD MARINADE

In a small bowl mix all ingredients together. Place fish in glass baking dish and add marinade. Cover and refrigerate several hours. Fish may be broiled or grilled. *Yield: 1 cup.*

1	CLOVE GARLIC, CRUSHED
1	TABLESPOON FRESH CILANTRO, CHOPPED
2	TEASPOONS SALT
¼	TEASPOON CAYENNE PEPPER
¼	CUP WHITE WINE VINEGAR
½	CUP DRY RED WINE
¼	CUP EXTRA VIRGIN OLIVE OIL

MARINADE FOR LAMB, PORK ROAST OR DUCK

In a large bowl combine garlic, cilantro, salt and cayenne. Stir in vinegar and wine. Slowly whisk in the olive oil. *Yield: 1 cup.*

NOTE: Meat should be marinated in refrigerator for 12 hours. Drain off marinade and chill for 2-3 hours before grilling.

2	TABLESPOONS BUTTER
1	TABLESPOON CHOPPED GARLIC
1	TEASPOON CHOPPED SHALLOT
4	FRESH JALAPEÑO PEPPERS, SEEDED AND MINCED
½	CUP CHICKEN STOCK
1	CUP WHIPPING CREAM SALT AND WHITE PEPPER TO TASTE
3	TABLESPOONS FRESH CILANTRO, CHOPPED
1	TABLESPOON FRESHLY SQUEEZED LIME JUICE

GREEN CHILI CREAM SAUCE

In a heavy saucepan melt butter. Add garlic, shallot and peppers. Cook until softened.

Add chicken stock and boil until reduced to 2 tablespoons. Add cream and simmer until sauce reduces by about a quarter and thickens slightly. Season to taste with salt and pepper.

Just before serving, reheat and stir in cilantro and lime juice. *Yield: 1 cup.*

NOTE: Serve with catfish, swordfish or warm smoked meats.

1	TEASPOON CHILI PASTE WITH GARLIC
½	TABLESPOON CHOPPED FRESH GINGER ROOT
¼	CUP TAMARI
½	TABLESPOON ORIENTAL SESAME OIL
1½	TABLESPOONS FRESHLY SQUEEZED LEMON JUICE
1½	TABLESPOONS SAKE

ORIENTAL DIPPING SAUCE FOR POULTRY OR SMOKED FISH

Place chili paste and ginger into a small bowl and slowly stir in tamari and then oil, lemon juice and sake. Let sit at room temperature for 1 hour. Stir before serving. *Yield: ¾ cup.*

4	POUNDS DARK PLUMS, WASHED, PITTED AND CHOPPED
1	CUP CHOPPED ONION
1	CUP GOLDEN RAISINS
2	TABLESPOONS ALLSPICE
2	TABLESPOONS BLACK PEPPERCORNS
2	TABLESPOONS MUSTARD SEED
½	TEASPOON CAYENNE PEPPER
1″	PIECE FRESH GINGER ROOT, PEELED, FINELY CHOPPED
2½	CUPS MALT VINEGAR
2	TABLESPOONS SALT
1¼	CUP FIRMLY PACKED BROWN SUGAR

PLUM SAUCE

In a pan combine plums, onion, raisins, spices, ginger root and 1¼ cups of the vinegar. Bring to a boil, reduce heat and simmer for 30 minutes or until plums are soft. Transfer mixture to food processor and blend.

Transfer sauce to a clean pan with remaining 1¼ cups vinegar and brown sugar. Heat to a boil and stir until sugar is dissolved. Reduce heat to simmer and cook for 1 hour, stirring occasionally, until sauce thickens. *Yield: 6 pints.*

NOTE: Serve heated as sauce for chicken, duck or other waterfowl or as a heated dip for Chinese egg rolls.

1	CUP SOY SAUCE
½	CUP DRY SHERRY
½	CUP SUGAR
½	CUP CATSUP
1	TEASPOON GARLIC POWDER
1	TEASPOON ONION POWDER
1	TEASPOON GROUND GINGER
1	TABLESPOON SESAME OIL
	STAR ANISE SPICE TO TASTE
	TOASTED SESAME SEEDS TO TASTE
	GREEN ONIONS, SLICED TO TASTE
1	TABLESPOON CORNSTARCH

SESAME SAUCE FOR BEEF

In a saucepan, combine all ingredients except cornstarch and heat to a boil. Lower heat and simmer 10 minutes, stirring occasionally. Thicken slightly with cornstarch mixed with 2 tablespoons cold water. *Yield: 2½ cups.*

NOTE: Use as marinade for beef or as a sauce on the side.

6	TABLESPOONS EXTRA VIRGIN OLIVE OIL
6	OIL-PACKED, SUN-DRIED TOMATOES, DICED
2	LARGE GARLIC CLOVES, MINCED
3-4	FRESH BASIL LEAVES
¾	TEASPOON SALT FRESHLY GROUND PEPPER TO TASTE
2	MEDIUM TOMATOES, CORED, SEEDED AND DICED

FRESH AND DRIED TOMATO TOPPING

In a skillet heat oil. Add sun-dried tomatoes, garlic, basil, salt and pepper and cook gently until garlic is soft, about 4 minutes.

Add fresh tomatoes to skillet and cook until heated through, about 1 minute. Adjust seasonings. *Yield: 1¼ cups.*

NOTE: Use on any basic Italian flat bread sprinkled with freshly grated Parmesan cheese and broiled.

¾	CUP SUNFLOWER SEEDS, SHELLED
1	CUP PACKED, FRESH BASIL LEAVES
1	CLOVE GARLIC
8	OUNCES GARLIC-FLAVORED GOAT CHEESE
1	TABLESPOON FRESHLY SQUEEZED LEMON JUICE
¼	CUP EXTRA VIRGIN OLIVE OIL FRESHLY GROUND PEPPER

SUNFLOWER-BASIL PESTO WITH GOAT CHEESE

Place sunflower seeds in a dry skillet. Cook over medium heat, stirring constantly, until lightly browned. Remove from skillet and cool.

Place seeds, basil leaves and garlic in a food processor. Process until mixture is a coarse paste. Add cheese, lemon juice and oil. Process until mixture is coarse sauce. Add pepper to taste. *Yield: 1 cup.*

NOTE: Excellent with pasta.

4	MEDIUM RED BELL PEPPERS, CORED, SEEDED AND CHOPPED
1	SMALL YELLOW ONION, CHOPPED
1	CLOVE GARLIC, CRUSHED PINCH HOT PEPPER FLAKES
1	TABLESPOON WALNUT OIL
1	TABLESPOON RED WINE VINEGAR
1	TABLESPOON FRESHLY SQUEEZED LEMON JUICE

RED PEPPER SAUCE

In a saucepan simmer all ingredients 30 minutes. Cool. Transfer mixture to a food processor and process until smooth. Strain. *Yield: 1 cup.*

NOTE: Serve warm with prawns.

THE WRIGLEY BUILDING, named for the family of chewing gum fame, was built in 1921 and is located on the northern bank of the Chicago River. An imposing structure with a distinctive clock tower, the building features baroque terra-cotta ornamentation that is highlighted by floodlights at night.

2 TABLESPOONS MINCED FRESH
    GINGER ROOT
1 SMALL CLOVE GARLIC, MINCED
4 TABLESPOONS SESAME
    SEED PASTE
2 TABLESPOONS PEANUT OIL
2 TEASPOONS ORIENTAL
    SESAME OIL
   SEVERAL DASHES HOT RED
    PEPPER SAUCE
1 TABLESPOON RICE VINEGAR
1 TEASPOON SUGAR
3 CUPS ROAST PORK, SHREDDED
4 PITA POCKETS
   BEAN SPROUTS
   SHREDDED LETTUCE

COLD PORK PITA POCKETS WITH BEAN SPROUTS

In a medium bowl, combine ginger, garlic, sesame seed paste, oils, pepper sauce, vinegar and sugar. Stir in pork and toss to coat well. Adjust seasonings.

Serve mixture in pita pockets with fresh bean sprouts and shredded lettuce. *Yield: 4 servings.*

2 TABLESPOONS UNFLAVORED
    GELATIN
1 CUP COLD WATER
2 CUPS CHICKEN BROTH, HEATED
2 CUPS MAYONNAISE
2 TEASPOONS FRESHLY SQUEEZED
    LEMON JUICE
2 TEASPOONS GRATED ONION
2 TEASPOONS CHOPPED CHIVES
   SALT AND FRESHLY
    GROUND PEPPER
   24 HARD-COOKED EGGS,
    FINELY CHOPPED
   SMALL SHRIMP AS GARNISH
   SLICED BLACK OLIVES
    AS GARNISH
   LORENZO DRESSING
12 OUNCES CHILI SAUCE
8 OUNCES FRENCH
    SALAD DRESSING
   JUICE OF 1 LEMON
1 TEASPOON SUGAR
⅓ CUP CHOPPED WATERCRESS

EGG MOUSSE WITH LORENZO DRESSING

For egg mousse, in a large bowl soften gelatin in cold water. Add hot chicken broth. Stir until dissolved. Stir in mayonnaise, lemon juice, onion, chives, salt and pepper. Add eggs. Stir and adjust seasonings. Pour mousse mixture into 12 individual oiled molds. Chill overnight.

For Lorenzo dressing, in a large container with a tightly fitting lid combine all ingredients. Shake well. Chill.

Unmold individual mousses onto serving plates. Serve with dressing and garnish with small shrimp and olive slices. *Yield: 12 servings.*

1	CUP FLOUR
¼	TEASPOON SALT
6	TABLESPOONS COLD UNSALTED BUTTER
1	TABLESPOON COLD WATER
2	TABLESPOONS CHARTREUSE LIQUEUR
2	THIN-SKINNED LEMONS, ENDS TRIMMED, SEEDED AND COARSELY CHOPPED
¾	CUP SUGAR
2	TABLESPOONS CHOPPED FRESH THYME
1	EGG FRESH HERBS FOR GARNISH

LEMON-HERB TARTLETS

In a bowl combine flour and salt. Cut in butter. Stir in water and 1 tablespoon of the Chartreuse. Form pastry into a ball. Wrap and chill 1 hour.

In a nonaluminum bowl combine lemons, sugar and thyme. Set aside 6 hours.

Divide pastry into 6 equal parts. Roll out and fit into six 3½″ tartlet tins. Freeze ½ hour. *Preheat oven to 375° F.*

Line tin bottoms with foil and fill with pie weights. Bake for 8 minutes. Remove weights and foil. Prick bottoms and bake 14 minutes longer or until golden.

In a bowl beat egg and remaining tablespoon Chartreuse. Stir into lemon mixture and spoon evenly into tartlet shells. Bake for 10-12 minutes or until set. Remove tartlets from tins to cool on rack. Garnish with fresh herbs. *Yield: 6 servings.*

NOTE: Quarter and serve with tea.

½	CUP CHOPPED ONION
1	POUND MUSHROOMS, CHOPPED
2	TABLESPOONS BUTTER
4	EGGS
1	CUP SOUR CREAM
1	CUP SMALL CURD COTTAGE CHEESE
1	CUP FRESHLY GRATED PARMESAN CHEESE
¼	CUP FLOUR
4	DROPS HOT RED PEPPER SAUCE
2	CUPS SHREDDED MONTEREY JACK CHEESE
6	OUNCES CRABMEAT, DRAINED

CRUSTLESS CRAB QUICHE

Preheat oven to 350° F. In a large saucepan, sauté onions and mushrooms in butter.

In a mixing bowl combine eggs, sour cream, cottage cheese, Parmesan cheese, flour and pepper sauce. Add mushroom and onion mixture, Monterey Jack cheese and crabmeat. Stir to combine.

Pour mixture into a buttered 10″ quiche dish and bake 40 minutes until golden brown. Let stand 15 minutes before serving. *Yield: 6 servings.*

12   EGGS
½   CUP BUTTER, SOFTENED
½   CUP FRESH CRABMEAT
½   CUP SWEET VERMOUTH, HEATED
      SALT AND FRESHLY GROUND
         PEPPER TO TASTE
½   CUP TOASTED
         SLIVERED ALMONDS

CRABMEAT SCRAMBLE WITH VERMOUTH

In a mixing bowl whisk eggs until well blended.

In top of double boiler, over simmering water, heat half of the butter. Pour in eggs and whisk until they just begin to set. Stir in remaining butter and crabmeat and continue cooking for about 15 minutes or until eggs are creamy.

Remove top of double boiler from heat and stir vermouth, salt and pepper into eggs. Spoon eggs onto serving plates, sprinkle with toasted almonds and serve immediately. *Yield: 4 to 6 servings.*

1½   CUPS SUGAR
½   TEASPOON CONFECTIONER'S
         SUGAR
½   TEASPOON CARDOMOM
4   WHOLE CINNAMON STICKS
2   TEASPOONS ORANGE ZEST
2   TEASPOONS LEMON ZEST
3   TABLESPOONS FRESHLY
         SQUEEZED LEMON JUICE
4   CUPS WATER
1   TEASPOON ALLSPICE
8   WHOLE CLOVES
1½   CUPS PITTED PRUNES
1⅓   CUPS DRIED FIGS, STEMS
         REMOVED AND HALVED
4   LARGE PEARS, CORED AND CUT
         INTO 1″ CUBES
4   LARGE APPLES, CORED AND CUT
         INTO 1″ CUBES
6   ORANGES, PEELED AND SLICED
4   BANANAS, PEELED AND SLICED
      SOUR OR WHIPPED CREAM
         AS GARNISH

WINTER CARNIVAL FRUIT COMPOTE

In a large saucepan combine sugar, powdered sugar, cardomom, cinnamon sticks, orange and lemon zests, lemon juice, water, allspice and cloves. Simmer, covered, 5 minutes.

Add prunes and figs. Simmer, covered, for an additional 5 minutes.

Stir in pears and apples. Cover and simmer 2 more minutes.

Uncover and cool. Once cooled, add the oranges and chill the mixture.

Add the bananas just before serving. Serve at room temperature with garnish of sour or whipped cream. *Yield: 24 servings.*

4	TABLESPOONS BUTTER
2	TABLESPOONS FLOUR
1	CUP HALF-AND-HALF
1½	CUPS GRATED EMMENTALER CHEESE
2	TABLESPOONS DRY WHITE WINE
	SALT AND HOT RED PEPPER SAUCE TO TASTE
1	BUNCH SCALLIONS, SLICED
9	OUNCES ARTICHOKE HEARTS, DRAINED, CUT IN HALF
6-8	OUNCES CRABMEAT
8	EGGS
	TOAST POINTS
	PARSLEY AS GARNISH

SCRAMBLED EGGS WITH ARTICHOKES AND CRAB

In a skillet, over medium heat, melt 2 tablespoons of the butter. Add flour and stir until smooth and thickened. Remove from heat. Add half-and-half in a slow steady stream, beating constantly. Return to heat and stir until sauce thickens. Add 1 cup of the cheese and stir until melted. Stir in wine, salt and pepper sauce. Cover with plastic wrap and set aside.

In another skillet place remaining 2 tablespoons butter and melt over medium heat. Add scallions and stir well. Cook 2 minutes. Add artichoke hearts and cook 4 more minutes. Remove mixture from heat and place on a large microwave-safe baking dish. Sprinkle crabmeat over artichoke mixture.

In a medium bowl beat eggs and pour over artichoke mixture. Cover with plastic wrap and microwave on high for 3 minutes. Stir cooked edge of eggs into center and stir in reserved cheese sauce. Microwave on medium power for 5 minutes, stirring after 3 minutes. Sprinkle remaining ½ cup cheese over top. Microwave uncovered, on medium power 1 minute, 30 seconds. Let stand 1-2 minutes until set. Serve over toast points and garnish with parsley. *Yield: 6 to 8 servings.*

2	EGGS, SEPARATED, ROOM TEMPERATURE
	PINCH OF SALT
	PINCH OF CREAM OF TARTAR
¼	CUP SUGAR
2	TABLESPOONS THAWED FROZEN ORANGE JUICE CONCENTRATE
1	TABLESPOON ORANGE-FLAVORED LIQUEUR
1½	TEASPOONS FLOUR
1	TEASPOON GRATED ORANGE PEEL
2	TABLESPOONS CONFECTIONER'S SUGAR
	SLICED RASPBERRIES, ORANGES OR STRAWBERRIES

ORANGE SOUFFLÉ OMELET

Preheat oven to 400° F. Butter an 8″ ovenproof skillet.

Beat egg whites with salt and cream of tartar until soft peaks form. Add ¼ cup sugar, 1 tablespoon at a time, and beat until eggs are stiff, not dry.

In another bowl beat yolks until thick and pale yellow. Add orange juice, liqueur, flour and orange peel. Gently fold in egg whites.

Spoon mixture into prepared skillet. Sift confectioner's sugar over top.

Bake 10-12 minutes until light brown. Garnish with fruit. *Yield: 1 serving.*

½	SMALL CUCUMBER, PEELED, SEEDED AND CHOPPED
	SALT
1	POUND SALMON FILLET, COOKED, FLAKED AND COOLED
2	TABLESPOONS CHOPPED FRESH DILL
4	TABLESPOONS MAYONNAISE
1	TABLESPOON FRESHLY SQUEEZED LEMON JUICE
½	TEASPOON WORCESTERSHIRE SAUCE
⅛	TEASPOON WHITE PEPPER
	SALT TO TASTE
6	SLICES PUMPERNICKEL OR DARK RYE BREAD
	BUTTER
6	SPRIGS FRESH DILL AS GARNISH

SALMON DILL CUCUMBER SANDWICHES

Place cucumber in a strainer, sprinkle with salt and toss. Press down to remove excess liquid.

In a bowl combine salmon, cucumber and dill.

In another bowl stir together mayonnaise, lemon juice, Worcestershire sauce, white pepper and salt to taste. Blend into salmon mixture.

Spread salmon on 3 of the bread slices and top with the other 3 slices that have been lightly buttered. Cut diagonally. Cover with a damp cloth to keep soft. Chill. Just before serving garnish each with a sprig of dill. *Yield: 6 sandwiches.*

1	EGGPLANT, CUT CROSSWISE INTO ½" THICK SLICES
1	LARGE TOMATO, SLICED ¼" THICK
½	POUND FRESH MOZZARELLA CHEESE, SLICED ¼" THICK
8	LARGE FRESH BASIL LEAVES FRESHLY GROUND BLACK PEPPER TO TASTE
½	CUP EXTRA VIRGIN OLIVE OIL

EGGPLANT SANDWICHES

Between 2 eggplant slices place 1 slice tomato, 1 slice mozzarella cheese and 1 basil leaf. Season with pepper and brush top and bottom of eggplant slices with olive oil.

Wrap individually in foil. Grill or broil 4"-6" from heat source 15-20 minutes or until hot and cheese has melted, turning once. *Yield: 6 to 8 sandwiches.*

12	SLICES WHITE BREAD
8	SLICES WHOLE WHEAT BREAD
2	TABLESPOONS MAYONNAISE
1	TEASPOON PREPARED MUSTARD
¼	CUP CHOPPED FRESH CHIVES
4	THIN SLICES HAM
4	OUNCES UNSALTED BUTTER, SOFTENED AND CREAMED
½	BUNCH WATERCRESS, STEAMED
⅓	CUP CHOPPED FRESH PARSLEY
18	THIN SLICES PEELED CUCUMBER
2	SLICES MONTEREY JACK CHEESE
1	TABLESPOON MANGO CHUTNEY
¼	CUP CHOPPED FRESH DILL
3	SLICES SMOKED SALMON

ENGLISH TEA SANDWICHES

For Ham Sandwich, in a small bowl mix together the mayonnaise and mustard and spread on 4 of the slices of white bread. Sprinkle with some of the chopped chives. Place the ham on 2 slices and cover with the other 2 slices of bread. Cut off the crusts. Cut each sandwich into 4 triangles and place on a plate under a dampened tea towel, until ready to serve.

For Watercress Sandwich, butter 4 slices of the white bread. Top with watercress. Cut and cover as above.

For Cucumber Sandwich, butter 4 slices of the white bread. Sprinkle with parsley. Top with 2 slices cucumber. Cut and cover as above.

For Cheese and Chutney Sandwich, sprinkle 4 slices of buttered whole wheat bread with parsley. Place the cheese on 2 slices and chutney on the other 2, and close. Cut and cover as above.

For Salmon Sandwich, sprinkle dill on 4 slices of buttered whole wheat bread. Top 2 bread slices with smoked salmon, cover with the other 2 slices. Cut and cover as above. *Yield: 56 tea sandwiches*

COMMITTEE LIST

ONE MAGNIFICENT COMMITTEE

Co-Chairperson
MARY ANN LILLIE

Co-Chairperson
LYNNE CLARK NORDHOFF

Production
AMANDA DE YOUNG

Internal Consulting Designer
KATIE JOHNSON

Recipes
KAREN Z. SMITH
SUZANNE GREEN STEVENS
MELISSA MCNEELY THOMPSON

Food Stylist
CARROLL BRENTON MICHALEK

Editor
LYNNE CLARK NORDHOFF

Underwriting
MARY KAY MCMAHON

Marketing
CONSTANCE T. TESKA

Promotion
JENNIFER SHRINER

Distribution
JOANNA BACON MORFORD

Sales
MARY ELLEN CONNELLAN
ADRIAN CULVER

Computer
MIMI BURKE

Index
NANCY LARUE

Treasurer
KAREN B. TAYLOR

Secretary
JANE SALISBURY HOGENCAMP
NANCY LARUE
PATTY LENTERS
JULIE MONTGOMERY

COMMITTEE MEMBERS

Carolyn Babcock
Louisa Bean Ciampi
Dana Boyajian
Mimi Burke
Betsy S. Collins
Mary Ellen Connellan
Carol McBurney Crowdus
Arian Culver
Amanda DeYoung
Jan Dougherty
Barbara Dubbs
Carrie Reavis Erzinger
Sara Flom
Christy Seip Fowler
Connie Frydenlund
Elsie Garbe
Paulette Gaudet
Leslie Geissler
Mary Ann Glunz
Barbara Gorham
Christiane Hansen
Susan M. Harris
Heidi Heller
Jody Krug Hillger
Jane Salisbury Hogencamp
Katie Johnson
Liz Keller
Wendy Rumsey Kilcollin
Jane Koleini
Deborah Gebhardt Kulp
Nancy LaRue
Dania Leon Leemputte
Patty Lenters
Mary Ann Lillie
Marjorie Maca
Mary Kay McMahon
Patty Mergener
Carroll Brenton Michalek
Julie Montgomery
Joanna Bacon Morford
Margie Newald
Lynne Clark Nordhoff
Julie Oberlin
Mary Eileen O'Donovan
Linda Pollack Pawelski
Anne H. Roberts
Betsy Rochman
Cindy Ross
Nellie Thoma Ross
Concy Ryan
Carol Sanders
Kara Schubel
Gigi Short
Jennifer Shriner
Karen Z. Smith
Jeannine Stadler
Julie Sowers

Suzanne Green Stevens
Martha Stone
Christie Swanson
Karen B. Taylor
Constance T. Teska
Melissa McNeely Thompson
Chris Tierney
Lisa Turley
Anne Forbes Wangman
Tracy Webb
Camille Weiss
Susan White
Mary Ann Zavell
Elizabeth Zimmer
Anne Zimmerman

THANK YOU!

THE JUNIOR LEAGUE OF CHICAGO IS GRATEFUL TO ITS MEMBERS AND MANY FRIENDS WHO CONTRIBUTED THEIR FAVORITE RECIPES. WE TRULY APPRECIATE YOUR ASSISTANCE WITH *ONE MAGNIFICENT COOKBOOK* AND WE HOPE WE HAVE NOT INADVERTENTLY EXCLUDED ANYONE.

RECIPE CONTRIBUTORS

Grace Aldworth
Pamela Anderson
Laura Ashcraft
Valerie Ault
Amy Baker
Barbara Belt
Pamela Bigelow
Anne Bird
Donna Boggs
Sue Bond
Sarah Bornstein
Sally Bradley
Nancy Buehler
Diane Burgess
Jeanne W. Smith Burke
Suzanne Butz
Sue Camins
Janie Campbell
Carla Sue Carstens
Jane Casper
Meg Chambers
Donna Chenoweth
Linda Blair Cline
P. Clough
P. Coladara
Anne Coladarci
Jane Coley
Mary Ellen Connellan
Debra Cook
Annie Coomer
Nan Cosier
Pamela Cramer
Carol Crowdus
Nanette Crowdus
Barbara Daley
Katie Detlefs
Carolyn De Grenier
Kitty Devers
Sharon Dixon
Beth Douglass
Hannah Duncan
Anne Economos
Nancy Jones Emrich
Mary Kay Enright
Bonnie Farlow
Mary Fields
Beverly Fisher
Ann Fitzgerald
Linda Forsberg
Christy Fowler
Bonita Friedland
Wendy Fuller
Elsie H. Garbe
Leslie Geissler
Mary Anne Glunz
Dorsey Skillern Gordon
Marilyn Gould
Josephine Graf
Polly Grafton

J. Douglas Gray
Wilsie Graybill
Betty Gunn
Mary Lois Hakewill
Mary Jane Hall
Susan Harris
Ginny Hartley
Molly Hayes
Susan Henderson
Mary J. Hill
Sally Hill
Jody Krug Hillger
Celia Hilliard
Connie Hodson
Randy Holgate
Marigay Horn
Diana Hubeny-McCall
Celia Hunt
Cynthia Hunt
Muffy Hunt
Paula Hunt
Maxine Hunter
Marilyn Isham
Ginny Istnick
Anne Jameson
Kathleen Jeffrey
Dana Johnson
Tava Jones
Gwen Judson
Gail Kahn
Mary Pat Kooi
Judy Kreamer
Beth Kress
Dale Krislov
Joan Krone
Jeanne Kuhn
Barbara Lamm
Mary Landis
Vlastimil Lebeda
Pamela Lee
Muffy Lewis
Mary Ann Lillie
Richard Lowe
Irene Lowry
Sophia Maass
Holly Madigan
Lisa Malkin
Ginny McEnerney
Mary Kay McMahon
Susan McNamara
Cathy McNulty
Nancy Mead
Susan Hill Mesrobian
Chris Middleton
Jean Middleton
Allona Mitchell
Diane Montani
Robert Montgomery
Weezie Monroe

Lisa Moore
Patti Morgenstern
Margo Moss
Mindy Munson
Nancy Myers
Polly Naumann
Susie Neaylon
Ruby Niesson
Muffy O'Connell
Mary Eileen O'Donovan
Elizabeth Oliver
Susan Olt
Kay O'Malley
Jane O'Neil
Christiane O'Neill
Susan Papadopulos
Caro Parsons
Nancy Patek
Susan Patterson
Linda Pawelski
Jody Pelletiere
Leslie Petter
Mary Ann Pillman
Hope Poor
Peggy Pool
Jane Power
Kay Proops
Betsy Pryser
Amy Puccinelli
Gayle Pucinski
Marion Randolph
Ruth Raths
Carrie Jo Reavis
Nancy Remington
Jeanette Reuben
Mary Jo Reynoldson
Jennifer Rielly
Devers Rinella
Gloria Rinella
Betsy Rochman
Joseph Rofferson
Cynthia Ann Ross
Nellie Ross
Stephanie Ross
Monique Rub
Kathy Ruff
Deborah Ryan
Christiane Saada
Carolyn Sanders
Mary Schaffernoth
Julie Schauer
Sherry Schellenbach
Victoria Schnure
Susan Schroeder
Leslie Shelton
Tara Shortly
Elizabeth Skalla
Mary Smart
Betsy Smith

RECIPE TESTERS

Jacqueline Smith
Karen Z. Smith
Nancy Spain
Jeannine Stadler
Diane Stanko
Nancy Stemwedel
Karen Sterling
Michelle Green Stevens
Suzanne Green Stevens
Liz Stiffel
Martha Stone
Gigi Belser Sturgis
Deborah Surpless
Helen Y. Sutter
Patricia Sutton
Michelle Sweeney
Sarah Taich
Maryanne Terrasse
Constance T. Teska
Melissa Thompson
Madeleine Toombs
Sherrie Travis
Kathy Tribby
Nancy Vaile
Ida Vaughan
Alice Venecek
Abbie Von Schlegell
Denise Vohnahme
Tracy Webb
Beverly Weber
Lisa Weismiller
Camille Weiss
Barbara Westover
Julie Whiting
Jane Asmuth Wienke
Kate Wiley
Sally Wille
Elizabeth Williams
Leah Wilson
Carol Woloson
Beth Wood
Charlene Yapp
Judy York
Lee Youngstrom
Lauren Zimmer
Nancy Zurkowski

IN MEMORIAM
Virginia Lorene Halpin

Pamela Anderson
Amy Jo Baker
Mary K. Baker
Susan Bankard
Susan Barkhausen
Marilyn Bartter
Julie Bauer
Sally Bradley
Laurel Bellows
Elizabeth Belt
Pamela Bigelow
Liz Blanchard
Mary Copes Bogash
Jamie Boltz
Sue Bond
Mindy Bourne
Nancy Bremner
Susan Brotman
Ellen Brumback
Janet Buckstein
Nancy Buehler
Betty Buerckholtz
Diane Burgess
Julia Burke
Mimi Burke
Debra Burtner
Suzanne Butz
Sue Camins
Jane Campbell
Julie Campbell
Missy Campbell
Laura Carriglio
Jennifer Carter
Jane Casper
Meg Chambers
Elizabeth Chandler
Linda Cline
Rebecca Cline
Anne Coladarci
Sara Colaianni
Elizabeth Cole
Jane Coley
Betsy S. Collins
Mary Ellen Connellan
Linda Cooper
Nan Cosier
Lisa Cottrell
Susan Craft
Pamela Cramer
Genie Cross
Wendy Cross
Carol Crowdus
Nanette Crowdus
Ann Dameron
Nancy Davies
Beth Davis
Ellen DeRose
Amanda DeYoung
Sandra Denny

Katie Detlefs
Amy Dickinson
Janice Dougherty
Beth Douglass
Sherrilyn Dubinsky
Hannah Duncan
Carol Ann Dunn
Denise Dwyer
Mary Carolyn Eaves
Jan W. Eichler
Mary Carolyn Embry
Kathy Elmer
Alison Farlow
Bonnie Farlow
Cathy Feehan
Katherine Alyn Feuer
Barbara L. Fields
Alease Osborne Fisher
Mary Kay Fordney
Linda Forsberg
Bonita Friedland
Constance Frydenlund
Victoria Galbraith
Elsie Helene Garbe
Ann Garnett
Anne Gately
Paulette Gaudet
Leslie Geissler
Virginia Gerst
Nancy Kelley Gibson
Kathryn Gilbertson
Dorsey Gordon
Polly Grafton
Carrie Grant
Terese Gravenhorst
Wilsie Graybill
Betty Gunn
Elizabeth Haire
M.J. Hall
Mary G. Harreld
Susan Harris
Mary Hayes
Susan Hays
Susan Heisler
Ann Helmer
Kathy Henricks
Leslie Herz
Mary Catherine Heylin
Kate S. Hill
Sara Hill
Jody Hillger
Constance S. Hodson
Jayne Hogan
Randy Holgate
Jeanne Honsinger
Susan Hoogland
Sheila Hoover
Jennifer Hubbard
Carol Huck

Alice Huff
Kay Hughes
Cynthia L. Hunt
Elizabeth Hunter
Lisa Ireland
Marilyn Isham
Mary Virginia Istnick
Mary Allison James
Anne Marie Jameson
Sarah Jelin
Mary Lou Jenkins
Mary Kathryn Johnson
Melanie Johnston
Tava Jones
Julie Joyce
Gwendolyn Judson
Mary Juers
Maura Junius
Gail Kahn
Dee Kane
Judy Keller
Liz Keller
Christine Kelly
Wendy Rumsey Kilcollin
Carol Kohlhaas
Jane Koleini
Beth Kress
Margaret Kristl
Dale Krislov
Victoria Kuhn
Joseph LaGivia, Jr.
Nancy W. LaRue
Rosemary Lakin
Mary Louise Lamberton
Mary L. Landis
Pamela Lee
Muffy Lewis
Mary Ann Lillie
Lisa Lindman
Wendy S. Lindner
Carolynn Lund
Mary Jennifer Lyons
Marjorie Maca
Lisa Klimley Malkin
Elizabeth Maloney
Melissa Mann
Sandra Martin
Barbara McBride
Maureen McDonagh
Hannah P. McInnis
Mary Kathryn McMahon
Lorel McMillan
Susan Pogue McNamara
Tracey McNeely
Catherine McNulty
Nancy Mead
Linda Meierdierks
Stephanie Mer
Donna Mitchell
Diane Montani

Julie Montgomery
Joanna Morford
Margo Nader
Polly Naumann
Susy Neaylon
Margaret Neff
Lisa Newell-Pollans
Lynne Clark Nordhoff
Marsha Nusslock
Elizabeth O'Connell
Mary Eileen O'Donovan
Sally O'Hara
Jane O'Neil
Christine O'Neill
Joan R. O'Neill
Elizabeth Oliver
Heidi Olsen
Susan Olt
Susan Papadopulos
Sally Parnell
Nora Partenheimer
Laura Pasek
Linda Pawelski
Martha Peterson
Nancy Petit
Leslie Petter
Mary Ann Pillman
Peggy Pool
Hope Poor
Sarah Powell
Kay Proops
Betsy Pryser
Carrie Joe Reavis
Karen Reyhan
Sandra Reyhan
Susan Rice
Jennifer Rielly
Anne Roberts
Tish Robinson
Betsy Rochman
Julie Rogers
Ellen Ross
Stephanie Ross
Joyce Rowell-McCarron
Marcia Rowley
Monique Rub
Katheryn Ruff
Suzanne Rutz
Christiane M. Saada
Naomi M. Sand
Carol Sanders
Louann Sanders
Julie Schauer
Ellen Marie Schenkel
Edith Schmid
Victoria Schnure
Mary Jane Schooley
Susan Schroeder
Kara Schubel
Carol M. Schulz

Adrienne Scott
Lindsay Scott
Mary Shanks
Elizabeth Sharp
Gigi Short
Louise Short
Mindy Simpson
Elizabeth Skalla
Carrie Smart
Mary Smart
Betsy Rodgers Smith
Jacqueline Smith
Jill Smith
Karen Z. Smith
Carla Snell
Susan Snider
Nancy N. Snyder
Pat M. Snyder
Nancy Spain
M. Jeannine Stadler
Cynthia Stanger
Diane Stanko
Lois Steans
Nancy Stemwedel
Bonnie Stern
Suzanne Green Stevens
Liz Stiffel
Corinne Stoker
Martha Stone
Martha Stouffer
Julie Strodel
Suzanne Strohschein
Cynthia A. Stuhley
Deborah Surpless
Sarah Taich
Sean-Ann Tangney
Maryanne Terrasse
Anita Thies
Marilynn Thoma
Melissa McNeely Thompson
Virginia Townley
Shelley Turley
Susan Underwood
Bernice C. Valantinas
Barbara A. Valicenti
Ann Vogl
Pamela Voss
Gail Walker
Anne Wangman
Tracy Webb
Martha Weber
Connie Weiss
Suzanne Wenk
Mariam Westin
Barb Westover
Susan White
Elizabeth Williams
Sheree Young
Lee Youngstrom

PHOTO CREDITS

INDEX

C